CREATE
IN ME
A HEART
OF
PEACE

Other Books from the (in)courage Community

DEVOTIONALS

Take Heart: 100 Devotions to Seeing God When Life's Not Okay
Empowered: More of Him for All of You

TRADE BOOKS

The Simple Difference by Becky Keife
Come Sit with Me (available November 2022)

BIBLE STUDIES

Courageous Simplicity: Living in the Simple Abundance of Jesus
Courageous Joy: Delight in God through Every Season
Courageous Influence: Embrace the Way God Made You for Impact
Courageous Kindness: Live the Simple Difference Right Where You Are

Create in Me a Heart of Hope
Create in Me a Heart of Peace
Create in Me a Heart of Wisdom (available January 2023)
Create in Me a Heart of Mercy (available May 2023)

For more resources, visit incourage.me

AN
(in)courage
BIBLE STUDY

CREATE IN ME A HEART OF PEACE

Becky Keife and the
(in)courage community

Revell
a division of Baker Publishing Group
Grand Rapids, Michigan

Published by Revell
a division of Baker Publishing Group
PO Box 6287, Grand Rapids, MI 49516-6287
www.revellbooks.com

Printed in the United States of America

Library of Congress Cataloging-in-Publication Data
Title: Create in me a heart of peace.
Description: Grand Rapids, MI : Revell, a division of Baker Publishing Group, [2022]
Identifiers: LCCN 2021035606 | ISBN 9780800738129
Subjects: LCSH: Peace—Religious aspects—Christianity—Textbooks.
Classification: LCC BV4908.5 .C73 2022 | DDC 248.4—dc23
LC record available at https://lccn.loc.gov/2021035606

Unless otherwise indicated, Scripture quotations are from the Christian Standard Bible®, copyright © 2017 by Holman Bible Publishers. Used by permission. Christian Standard Bible® and CSB® are federally registered trademarks of Holman Bible Publishers.

Scripture quotations labeled MSG are from THE MESSAGE, copyright © 1993, 2002, 2018 by Eugene H. Peterson. Used by permission of NavPress. All rights reserved. Represented by Tyndale House Publishers, Inc.

Scripture quotations labeled NIV are from THE HOLY BIBLE, NEW INTERNATIONAL VERSION®, NIV® Copyright © 1973, 1978, 1984, 2011 by Biblica, Inc.® Used by permission. All rights reserved worldwide.

Scripture quotations labeled NLT are from the *Holy Bible*, New Living Translation, copyright © 1996, 2004, 2007, 2013, 2015 by Tyndale House Foundation. Used by permission of Tyndale House Publishers, Inc., Carol Stream, Illinois 60188. All rights reserved.

Italics added to Scripture quotations reflect the author's emphasis.

(in)courage is represented by Alive Literary Agency, www.aliveliterary.com.

Baker Publishing Group publications use paper produced from sustainable forestry practices and post-consumer waste whenever possible.

22 23 24 25 26 27 28   7 6 5 4 3 2 1

CONTENTS

INTRODUCTION

Does the idea of lasting peace seem like an impossible dream?

When you turn on the evening news and hear of another mass shooting, when that person you were supposed to rely on proved untrustworthy again, when you scroll social media and are bombarded by digital finger-pointing, name-calling, and shame-blaming, it's easy to feel that peace is elusive. It's easy to believe that peace is something mythical reserved for fairy tales and one-week summer vacations, that peace can't reach inside oncology wards and broken relationships.

We all want peace. We crave an inner calm-meets-strength that doesn't rattle with volatile circumstances or disappear with busyness.

What if I told you this kind of unshakable peace actually is possible?

Create in Me a Heart of Peace will guide you to discovering the life-changing power of God's peace. Not a peace reserved for Sunday mornings or when you remember to pray before bed, but a peace that's available to you right now, right where you are. God wants to reach into your heart with His peace when you're exhausted from rocking a colicky baby or when you're weary of being single. He wants to comfort you with His peace when you're enduring another day of chronic illness or facing a conflict without a clear resolution. True peace isn't a fable or a religious fabrication to make people simply feel better; true peace is a *person* named Jesus.

You might already know Him, but I guarantee there is more He has for you, more He wants you to experience as His beloved friend, lamb, and daughter.

Together we will learn that God is our unwavering, never-ending source of peace and that His peace is also an invitation to partner with Him. Peace is a *posture* we learn to live with and a *promise* we learn to cling to. Peace is a *practice* by which we shape the rhythm of our days, and it's an *outpouring* of the Spirit we get to experience. And finally, peace is our *purpose*, our calling as children of God to join the Father in His work of bringing peace on earth as it is in heaven.

This isn't a journey for the super-spiritual or those who seemingly have it all together. *Create in Me a Heart of Peace* is for anyone who longs to know that God is real and present and constantly working on our behalf. Whether you've been reading the Bible for decades or you're just finding out what it means to know Jesus, these pages are available to you as a guide to help you move through Scripture and discover what God's Word says about peace and the difference it can make in your life.

How to Use This Study

Create in Me a Heart of Peace is designed to be used by individuals or small groups. For groups doing this study, I recommend allowing at least forty-five minutes for discussion (or more for larger groups).

As you work through this study, take your time. Let God's Word minister to your soul. Don't be afraid to ask hard questions, write out your doubts, or wrestle through something you're not sure about. This is your space to be honest with God and to hear from Him. I believe He has something personal and specific to say to you on each day.

Rather than being one more thing on your to-do list, I pray that this study can be an encouraging, life-giving experience that draws you closer to God as you encounter the hope of His Word and the peace of

His presence. If you don't get to every question, don't stress! This is a pressure-free zone. Work through this study at your own pace. Invest the fifteen intentional minutes you have each day, or linger over every lesson for an hour or more. Either way, ask God to reveal His insight and truth to you. Then listen as He speaks to you through His Word.

> ▶ Enhance your community study experience with the *Create in Me a Heart of Peace* leader guide from (in)courage. Go to www.incourage.me/leaderguides to download your FREE small group resources.

Each week of this study will begin with a personal story from an (in)courage writer— a woman like you who is willing to "go first" with her hard, messy, real story. Many of these stories begin in deep heartache but inevitably find their way back to God and His profound gift of peace. Each week will also provide a memory verse (or verses) to work on throughout the study, to tether your heart to the peace of Christ long after you close this book.

As you go through this study, you will find it helpful to have a Bible or a Bible app for reading Scripture, as well as a journal for writing each week's memory verse(s). (That "journal" doesn't have to be anything fancy, though. A simple notebook will work just fine!)

The first day of each week will focus on one personal story and introduce that week's memory verse(s) . The following four days will dive deep into God's Word, illustrating the various reasons we need peace, where we find it, and the difference it will make in our lives.

Are you ready? Your (in)courage sisters and I are excited to go on this journey with you. Together we'll encounter God's living Word in new ways as we learn to let His peace permeate every thought in our minds, every word on our tongues, and every meditation of our hearts. The peace of Jesus is more powerful, practical, and applicable to our lives than any counterfeit version our culture could offer.

God is ready to create in you a heart of peace. Open your heart and get ready for Him to do more than you could dream.

PEACE IS A PERSON

If the world was trying to sell peace, it might give us a brochure with sunset beaches and umbrella drinks. We might see a commercial depicting happy families, big homes, and successful careers followed by tranquil music and towel-clad women receiving spa treatments. The world's version of peace in the form of financial security and tropical vacations might be enticing, but that temporary pleasure is not the same as true peace.

When the doctor calls with a devastating diagnosis, when the one you thought was trustworthy betrays you, when the stress of regular life simply pushes you to your limit—only one person can provide peace in the midst of it all. His name is Jesus. This week we will be looking at the ways the person of Jesus is the source of unwavering peace. From His birth to His death, from the beginning of time to eternity in heaven, we'll discover how peace is possible only through Him.

Today I share a story that describes a time in my life when I realized the world's security was fleeting and I needed a firmer foundation to build my life on. I needed the peace of Jesus. As you read, think about how God has used seasons of disappointment or heartache in your life to draw you closer to Him.

A Story of Peace

It happened more than twenty years ago, but I remember it like it was yesterday. The ring of our dorm phone jolted me from a deep sleep.

My roommate reached over and picked up the beige receiver. "Hello?" Sarah said in a froggy voice. I rolled over on my top bunk in annoyance—*my one morning without an early class!*

After a brief minute, Sarah hung up the phone and said, "That was my mom. There's been a terrorist attack."

The words hadn't even registered when Sarah turned on our tiny box TV. We watched as a second airplane crashed into the Twin Towers on the live broadcast. My mouth fell open but no words came out. I couldn't comprehend what I was witnessing.

As the news slowly spread throughout the dorms (this was long before the days of smartphones and social media), so did a sense of panic. RAs came knocking on doors announcing that classes were canceled and the entire campus was shutting down out of an abundance of caution. We were on the opposite coast, but could another attack be coming? Would Los Angeles also be targeted?

The phone lines were jammed, so I pulled on a T-shirt and a crumpled pair of jeans and walked to the building next door to see my boyfriend. We congregated in the dim hallway with a couple other friends from our college ministry group. After sharing our shock and fear, someone finally said, "We should pray." So there on the dingy carpet, with fellow students coming and going, we sat and prayed. For those trapped in the burning skyscrapers. For the first responders and everyone who inhaled the ominous gray plume of ash and debris we watched sweep through Manhattan's streets. We asked the Spirit to groan for that which our group of nineteen- and twenty-year-olds had no words.

Eventually, our small gathering dispersed, leaving just me and my boyfriend. His eyes revealed a troubled soul. Two girls walked by with puffy red eyes. Everyone was shaken by what was happening. "Do you want to come back to my room so we can watch the news with Sarah and see what's going on?" I asked.

"No, but I would like to go somewhere . . . just us. To talk. How about the beach?"

I felt shaky in my core. *Terrorism was something in foreign countries with rogue governments and unstable economies,* I naively thought. *How could this be happening here?* With classes canceled, sitting on the sand with the soothing soundtrack of waves sounded perfect.

We headed out to his rusty blue pickup truck, but one look at the parking lot told us we weren't going anywhere. With an evacuation order in effect for all staff and students not living on campus, the parking lot was a zoo! Lines of cars extended in a tangled pattern across the sprawling university. Every exit was jammed.

He grabbed my hand and we hiked up the long, paved hill toward upper campus, which was now almost completely deserted. The image of that plane piercing the building kept playing in my mind. I couldn't swallow the lump in my throat.

At least we're together, I thought, squeezing my guy's hand. *No matter what happens, we can face it side by side.*

We finally stopped on the grassy knoll near the north traffic circle. A weeping willow bowed its branches away from a brick office, offering us a crescent cocoon of shade. He put his arm around me, and I leaned my head on his shoulder. We sat in comfortable silence, best friends not needing to fill the undeniable void of pain and confusion of this historic day.

Finally, my boyfriend shifted his body to turn toward me and inhaled a deep breath. I was eager to hear his sensitive and insightful thoughts on the attack. But instead he told me we needed to break up.

Breath left my lungs like I'd been punched in the gut. Again, I felt disoriented, unable to grasp what was happening. He was *the one.* The one who stole my heart with his dimples and curly hair. The one who earned my trust with his unfailing honesty and integrity. We shared the same major and served together on our ministry leadership team. Every picture of the future I envisioned had a ring on my finger and his arm around my waist. I loved him. How could this be happening?

We talked and cried until there was nothing left to say. I couldn't change his mind. I couldn't fix it or turn back time. We walked slowly back to the dorms and said goodbye.

I spent the rest of that day and night in bed. The news played constantly in the background, giving updates on the rising death toll and emerging details of the terrorists' coordinated attacks. My eyes ached from crying, and I felt a physical pain in my heart. All sense of safety and security had vanished. My future was a shattered mess of broken dreams. It felt like a brick pressed on my chest. It was hard to breathe.

One morning a few weeks later, I opened my Bible after another sleepless night. I didn't even know what to read, so I opened to John because it was familiar. I skimmed a few passages, and then a word jumped out from the page like a 3D special effect. *PEACE*.

"Peace I leave with you. My peace I give to you. I do not give to you as the world gives. Don't let your heart be troubled or fearful" (John 14:27).

In the aftermath of 9/11 and in the wake of that devastating breakup, God was inviting me to change the way I defined peace and change where I looked for it. Living in a prosperous first-world country is no guarantee of peace. Peace doesn't come from titles like boyfriend and girlfriend. Peace is not found in relationships or plans unfolding according to my dreams. That heartbreaking September showed me that the peace the world gives is temporary, circumstantial, fallible.

But God offers a different kind of peace. Lasting. Unshakable. Perfect. When the whole world fractures or my own life shatters, the peace of Jesus is still available because the person of Jesus never changes.

Whether we're in a time of crisis or just trudging through the struggles of ordinary life, we can entrust our troubled, fearful hearts to the one who is worthy of our trust.

—BECKY KEIFE

Can you recall a time when you were shaken to your core? Describe that season or situation and what it felt like to lack peace.

_____

_____

_____

_____

John 14 records part of what Jesus told His disciples at their last meal together before His arrest and crucifixion. Read verses 1–4. Why do you think Jesus chose to include this in His final encouragement to His friends? How does maintaining an eternal perspective affect your peace?

_____

_____

_____

_____

Read Psalm 46:1–3. How is God's presence related to our fear of trouble? What comfort or encouragement do these verses give you?

_____

_____

_____

_____

SCRIPTURE MEMORY MOMENT

This week's memory verse is John 14:27. Write out the verse in your journal (as printed here from the CSB or from your favorite translation). Throughout the week, commit these words to memory as you ask God to create in you a heart of peace centered on Jesus, the person of peace.

Peace I leave with you. My peace I give to you. I do not give to you as the world gives. Don't let your heart be troubled or fearful.

A PRAYER FOR TODAY

DEAR JESUS, *thank You for offering a peace so different from what the world gives. Without You, my heart would be perpetually troubled. Fear would be a constant companion. I acknowledge that I can't control my circumstances or strive for peace. I surrender my life and heart to You. Please use this study and time in Your Word to create in me a heart of peace. Amen.*

Look! The virgin will conceive a child!
    She will give birth to a son,
and they will call him Immanuel,
    which means "God is with us."
                    Matthew 1:23 NLT

When have you felt God's presence with you? Describe that experience here.

_____

_____

_____

_____

The Old Testament is full of prophecies about Christ—the Messiah, the promised redeemer of the Israelites. The Hebrew word *mashiach* (messiah) means "anointed one" or "chosen one." He would be the one chosen to right all wrongs, to forever bridge the gap of sin and restore God's people to right relationship with Him.

One of the most familiar Old Testament prophecies is found in Isaiah 9:6 (NIV):

> For to us a child is born,
>   to us a son is given,
>   and the government will be on his shoulders.

> And he will be called
>> Wonderful Counselor, Mighty God,
>> Everlasting Father, Prince of Peace.

Every December, Christians sing these famous words to the tune from Handel's *Messiah*. The words flow out of our mouths in triumphant declaration, but do we stop to think what exactly it means for this promised child to be the Prince of Peace? What peace does He possess? What peace does He offer?

No doubt you've discovered through the ups and downs of life that true peace is not just a calm feeling, because feelings can be fleeting. Nor is it favorable circumstances, which can suddenly shift, or simply the lack of chaos, which can emerge at any time.

But what *is* peace then? Peace can be described as an experience, a gift, and a practice, yes. But at its foundation, peace is a person.

Have you ever thought about the name "Prince of Peace"? What qualities or characteristics do you think it embodies that are different from the other names listed in Isaiah 9:6?

Read Matthew 1:18–25. Note how verse 23 is quoting the prophet Isaiah (Isa. 7:14). What does the name "Immanuel" mean? Of all the names God could have chosen for His Son, why do you think He chose Immanuel?

_____

_____

Immanuel. God is with us! What greater peace can we find than knowing God's presence is with us? Let your mind wander through that unfathomable wonder and miracle.

The God who knows the grains of sand that stretch across every desert and shore. The God who counts the wispy hairs on each baby's head. The God who formed earth, sky, and sea with the power of His words. The God who breathed life into humanity. *That* God. The Almighty. Who was and is and is to come. *He* was sent to earth through the womb of a young woman to be *with us*.

If you're looking for peace in your bank account balance or the embrace of a significant other, if you're relying on political policies, landing your dream job, or your mother-in-law finally accepting you in order to have peace—oh, friend. You will be disappointed and tangled in fear and worry again and again. There's nothing wrong with wanting a meaningful job, a sound government, and healthy relationships. But we cannot allow those things to rule us and dictate our peace.

Centuries before Jesus was born of a virgin, He was called *Sar-Shalom*, the Prince of Peace. *Sar* is the Hebrew word translated as "prince," and it refers to a ruler, a person in authority, a commander, the head, someone of noble birth. *Yes, this is Jesus.*

Shalom is the Hebrew word translated as "peace" and means "completeness, soundness, welfare." *Yes, this is Jesus.*

Immanuel. God is with us! What greater peace can we find than knowing God's presence is with us?

Jesus, the Messiah, the Prince of Peace, was sent by a loving God for
the sake of our spiritual welfare in order to complete—make whole—
that which had been broken in humanity.

**Where in your life does your welfare feel uncertain? What is lacking or
fractured that needs to be made complete?**

_____

_____

_____

_____

I don't know about you, but there are several names of Jesus that feel
comfortable to me. I'm at ease calling Him *Savior* and *Shepherd*. It
feels natural to call Him *Lord* and even *Friend*. But never has *Prince*
rolled off my tongue in prayer or natural conversation.

Yet consider this: A prince rules. A prince has authority. A prince is
subject to his father—the king. What a beautiful and apt description of
who the Son of God is in relationship to us and to His Father. The pair-
ing of *prince* and *peace* further reveals God's heart for His people—His
heart for you and me. His authority over our lives isn't motivated by a
desire for power or a self-serving agenda. He's not a ruler who wants to
control you; He's a ruler who wants to invite you into the life of peace
only He can provide.

**Slowly read Psalm 145. How does this psalm affirm the picture of Jesus
as the Prince of Peace? Record a couple of verses that stand out to you.**

_____

_____

_____

_____

SCRIPTURE MEMORY MOMENT

Write out John 14:27. How has God given you peace recently? Now text this verse to a friend who might be encouraged by it. Invite her to memorize it with you!

A PRAYER FOR TODAY

JESUS, *Prince of Peace. Thank You for coming into this world to give something the world cannot provide—true peace. Prepare my heart to learn. Prepare my mind to understand the truth You reveal in Scripture. I give You full authority over my life. Lead me and guide me and create in me a heart of peace today. Thank You for being with me. Amen.*

DAY 3

Glory to God in the highest heaven,
and peace on earth to people he favors!

Luke 2:14

What comes to mind when you hear the words "peace on earth"? When you look at your life and the world, where do you see a need for more peace?

_____

_____

_____

_____

In your mind's eye, travel to an open field on a dark night. You don't see any city lights, just the twinkling of stars and the reflection of the moon illuminating a group of shepherds watching their sleeping flocks. The night is silent save for the sound of crickets and the occasional bleating of a sheep stirring in its sleep.

Suddenly, an angel appears. The shepherds tremble and shield their eyes from the brilliant light as the glory of the Lord shines around them. Just imagine how they must have felt seeing something so unexpected, so incredible!

> But the angel said to them, "Don't be afraid, for look, I proclaim to you good news of great joy that will be for all the people: Today in the city of David a Savior was born for you, who is the Messiah, the Lord. This will be the sign for you: You will find a baby wrapped tightly in cloth and lying in a manger." (Luke 2:10–12)

This, of course, is the first proclamation that the promised Messiah had arrived. After centuries of waiting, the Savior was here. Perhaps you've heard this story read every Christmas for as many years as you've been alive. It's easy for something so familiar to become commonplace. But there is nothing ordinary about this story!

How does the angel describe this news, and who was it for?

_____

_____

Long before Jesus was born, God selected the Israelites as His chosen people—a portion of humanity to represent God's love for all creation. Jesus was the fulfillment of God's plan to restore relationship with everyone, with "all the people," as the angel proclaimed. Does anything in your past or present make you feel disqualified from receiving this good news, from accepting God's love? Read John 3:16–18 and write down what you observe.

_____

_____

_____

_____

Back in the field, before the shepherds could fully process what the angel had said to them, a huge heavenly assembly appeared, praising God. And what exactly did they say? "Glory to God in the highest heaven, and peace on earth to people he favors!" (Luke 2:14).

If I'm honest, this is where my imagination usually inserts some Christmas garland and angelic children in choir robes. The scene becomes part of a holiday montage in my mind, and in the swirl of pageantry, I forget to consider what these powerful words actually mean.

"Glory to God in the highest heaven." The first thing that pours from the lips of this group of heaven-sent beings is praise. They worship God and turn their focus to Him, as if to say, "Everything that is happening is all about Him! God deserves all the credit and praise!" What a model for us today.

Immediately following that, they declare, "And peace on earth to people he favors." They go from glorifying God to immediately declaring the peace He offers us through Jesus. The heavenly host didn't say "peace to the Israelites" or "peace to perfect people." No! They declared "peace on *earth*." It's an echo of what the Lord's angel had just said—that this good news was for *all* people. God favors all people because He gives all people the opportunity to know Him and be saved through Jesus.

What do you think is the significance of peace being the first attribute broadcast about Jesus, the promised Messiah?

We need peace on earth in the face of homelessness and hopelessness. We need peace to face the horrors of human trafficking and mental illness. And most of all, we need the peace and power of Christ in the face of our own sin.

It's probably not hard for you to see the need for peace—in your own life and in the world around you. In my opening story, I shared one historic day of seeing the chaos, disillusionment, brokenness, and heartbreak of this world, which has only been reinforced in the decades since. We live in a world marked and marred by prejudice and injustice, sickness and betrayal. Chances are, you or someone you love has suffered through cancer or addiction, natural disasters or disasters of their own making. We need peace on earth in the face of homelessness and hopelessness. We need peace to face the horrors of human trafficking and mental illness. And most of all, we need the peace and power of Christ in the face of our own sin.

Romans 3:23 says it clearly: "For all have sinned and fall short of the glory of God." The reality of the fall is all around us. But that's not the end of the story!

"But God is so rich in mercy, and he loved us so much, that even though we were dead because of our sins, he gave us life when he raised Christ from the dead. (It is only by God's grace that you have been saved!)" (Eph. 2:4–5 NLT).

The angel's good news for all people resulted in a way for each of us to be restored. Peace on earth and peace for eternity! The apostle Paul makes it crystal clear for believers so that no one will get confused: "God saved you by his grace when you believed. And you can't take credit for this; it is a gift from God. Salvation is not a reward for the good things we have done, so none of us can boast about it" (Eph. 2:8–9 NLT).

"Peace on earth," the angels proclaimed on the day of Jesus's birth. There is no peace in striving. No peace in trying to earn your salvation. No peace in wondering if you followed the rules closely enough or offered the right sacrifices. No peace in hoping your good deeds outweigh your bad.

The peace of Christ is in knowing that you are loved by God so much that He filled in the gap of all your mistakes with His grace. God's Son, born of a woman, lived a sinless life and submitted to a brutal death on a cross in order to be the bridge of peace. You don't have to earn it or work for it. It's already yours—you are a favored one. He is offering you a gift so amazing that a multitude of angels filled a silent night with the good news.

> Read Ephesians 2:1–10. Consider the reality of your sin and the miraculous gift of Jesus. How does thinking about God's love through Christ give you peace? If you've never accepted God's gift of grace and put your trust in Jesus, you can do so today.

SCRIPTURE MEMORY MOMENT

Read and write John 14:27 three times. Consider how this passage fits with the angels' declaration.

A PRAYER FOR TODAY

DEAR GOD, *thank You for loving me and caring for this weary world so much that You sent Your Son to bring peace to earth and save us from our sins. I've fallen short in a thousand different ways. I'm so grateful I don't have to earn Your love or seek peace on my own. I receive Your gift of grace and I give You glory! Keep turning my heart to You. Amen.*

Jesus replied, "If you only knew the gift God has for you and who you are speaking to, you would ask me, and I would give you living water."

John 4:10 NLT

In what area of your life are you lacking peace? When do you find yourself turning to what the world offers instead of turning to Jesus?

With the afternoon sun high overhead, Jesus sat beside a stone well and asked a woman for a drink. The presence of another person at this time of day surely must have startled her. She was used to drawing water alone. That's why she deliberately went to the well at noon. She was also taken aback that a Jewish man would speak to her, a Samaritan woman. Such a thing was way outside traditional social decorum, given their differences in ethnicity and gender. But Jesus was rarely interested in maintaining societal expectations.

Perplexed by Jesus's presence and His request, the woman questions, "Why are you asking me for a drink?"

Jesus replies, "If you only knew the gift God has for you and who you are speaking to, you would ask me, and I would give you living water" (John 4:9–10 NLT).

Yeah, that clears things up . . . *not so much*. Is Jesus trying to confuse her? No. He is trying to get her—and each of us—to throw what we *think* we know out the window and open our hearts to a new and deeper understanding of what we really need and who can really give it.

Read John 4:1–26. Why do you think Jesus points out the woman's past marriages and her current relationship with a man who isn't her husband? How do you think the woman felt about Jesus having such intimate knowledge of her life?

Read verse 15 again. Can you relate to this feeling of wanting a permanent solution for your thirst? When have you felt spiritually parched—or are you thirsty today? Share how that feels.

The Samaritan woman had tried to quench her thirsty soul with the temporary affection of men, only to end up unsatisfied again and again. She isn't the only one who has looked for fulfillment in all the wrong places. God's own people did this repeatedly.

In Jeremiah 2:13, the Lord declares, "My people have committed two sins: They have forsaken me, the spring of living water, and have dug their own cisterns, broken cisterns that cannot hold water" (NIV). He uses objects familiar to the prophet's audience to describe Israel's spiritual condition. These words also have great significance and application for us today. To begin, God is assessing the actions and faith of His people. He's calling them out and naming how they have strayed from His will.

The Hebrew word translated here as "forsaken" is *azab*, which means "to leave, neglect, refuse, or abandon." It wasn't that the Israelites were simply slacking on their prayer time or hadn't followed one tiny detail of Jewish law. They had *abandoned* their faith in the one true God, which goes directly against the first two commandments God gave His people through Moses: "Do not have other gods besides me" and "Do not make an idol for yourself" (Exod. 20:3–4).

God describes Himself as a spring of living water. For the original audience, this brought to mind an actual spring. Often called an artesian spring, this rare natural phenomenon brings water continually to the surface from deep underground. In Jeremiah's day, an artesian spring was more valuable than gold! Homes didn't have a kitchen sink, bathroom sink, washing machine, dishwasher, shower, bathtub, or backyard hose. Without modern plumbing and running water like we're blessed with in developed countries today, collecting, storing, and retrieving water was no joke. Finding and storing water took an incredible amount of time and effort. But a spring of living water provided all the water needed without any of the work.

Water is a life source. We literally cannot live without it. So for people in Jeremiah's time, a living spring was a gift not to be taken for granted. God is just like this. He is the one true, unending source of life and peace. He offers pure, life-sustaining refreshment like nothing else can. When the hardships of life leave us parched, too dry and weary to continue, the peace of God is refreshing soul nourishment that empowers us to keep on keeping on.

> Read Jeremiah 2:13 again. Imagine living in a time or a place where running water is not available. Would you ever bypass a pure, free-flowing spring in favor of digging your own well? How does this illustration apply to your spiritual life?

You might be wondering, *What's a cistern?* A cistern is a holding tank for water that is dug into the ground. The water inside a cistern is still, unmoving. In juxtaposition to "living water," this water is dead.

A cistern is intended to be leakproof. But what happens when the lining cracks or the internal structure breaks? It can no longer hold water. Adding more water to a broken cistern is futile. Expecting a broken cistern to provide life-giving water is pointless.

It would be unthinkable for a person to walk past a bubbling artesian spring of clean water and instead choose to exert tremendous energy digging and filling a cistern in order to draw from the stagnant water source. It just wouldn't make sense. Yet this is exactly what the people of Israel had done in their spiritual lives.

This is exactly what we often do in our own lives. And it grieves the heart of God.

"They have forsaken me." Can you hear the anguish and disappointment in those words? Being refused and abandoned by His chosen people brought great pain to God's heart. He feels the same way when we turn away from Him today.

We may not worship statues made of gold or call on the name of foreign gods like the people in Jeremiah's time, but have you ever put your trust in something or someone other than Jesus? Think about it. Where do you go for purpose, significance, and security? Where do you turn when you're thirsty for truth and yearning for peace?

As I examine my own heart before the Lord, I have to admit that at times I'm not so unlike the Israelites. I can forget all that God has done to rescue me from bondage, forgive my sins, and invite me into a relationship of love and freedom with Him. I can slip into the trap of believing that other water sources, other life sources, are just as good and satisfying as God.

Some of my cisterns look like Instagram scrolling and seeking satisfaction from the stale water of likes and comments. I've dug cisterns of relationships and work projects—returning again and again to something that has value but was never intended to be an endless source of nourishment and fulfillment.

Maybe you've dragged your thirsty soul to the cisterns of online shopping or too many glasses of wine. Maybe you've neglected the living spring of God for the broken wells of politics, self-help books, the latest fad diet, or your bank account balance.

When you're scared and confused, do you rush to God and the living spring of His Word for wisdom and truth, or are you quick to turn on the news or ask a friend's advice? When you're lonely and longing to feel loved, do you ask the Spirit of our living God to surround you and minister to you, or do you reach for that tub of ice cream or the arms of someone who isn't your husband? When you're anxious and hurting, do you run to the Living Water, the Prince of Peace in prayer, or do you rush to Facebook, Amazon, or a romance novel?

Friends, it's time to recognize the cisterns we've dug. It's time to confess that we've habitually visited these leaky, polluted cisterns. It's time to choose living water.

> **Read Isaiah 48:17–18. What is God asking you to do today? How would obeying Him lead you to overflow with His peace?**

SCRIPTURE MEMORY MOMENT

Read John 14:27 and write it three times in your journal. Thank God for offering you the living water of Jesus.

A PRAYER FOR TODAY

JESUS, *thank You for offering peace that does not run dry. I confess I've looked for life and contentment apart from You. I've found temporary pleasure and satisfaction but never the enduring peace and freedom I long for. Life is in You! Teach my heart to choose You every moment of every day. May Your peace overflow in my life. Amen.*

DAY 5

I have told you all this so that you may have peace in me.
Here on earth you will have many trials and sorrows. But take
heart, because I have overcome the world.

John 16:33 NLT

What trials or sorrows are weighing you down today? Now pause and
pray. Open your hands and offer your burdens to God. Picture Him holding them and offering you His peace in return.

I wonder if the disciples gave each other the side eye when Jesus told
them that here on earth they would have many trials and sorrows. Did
they think of the families and jobs they had left to follow Jesus? Did
they think of their friend John the Baptist who had been beheaded for
his faith? Did they remember the faces of every sick or bleeding or
demon-possessed person who had come to Jesus over the last three
years seeking healing?

Surely the disciples were as keenly aware of the trials and sorrows of
this world as you and I are today. They may not have known words like

cancer, coronavirus, terrorism, or *depression,* but they saw corruption in the temple courts, watched parents grieve the death of children, and knew that some people would rather murder the promised Messiah than surrender their grasp on power. And they probably sensed that things were going to get worse before they got better. Have you had that sinking feeling too?

On the last night before He was crucified, Jesus lingered around a table with His closest friends and poured out His heart. Though they had logged countless hours and miles doing life and ministry side by side, Jesus used this night, known as the Last Supper, to *make sure* they knew the most important things.

Jesus's farewell teaching is recorded in John 13–16. His final instructions fall under three main themes:

- Love one another (13:34–35; 15:17).
- If you love God, obey Him and remain in Him to bear fruit (14:15; 15:5–10).
- God will send the Spirit to guide you (14:26; 16:7–14).

It's at the end of this rich, mind-bending, life-changing, revolutionary teaching that Jesus says, "I have told you all this so that you may have peace in me. Here on earth you will have many trials and sorrows. But take heart, because I have overcome the world" (John 16:33 NLT).

Consider the three main themes of Jesus's farewell teaching. Look up the verses listed above. How might loving others, loving and obeying God, and receiving the Holy Spirit lead to a life of peace?

_____

_____

_____

_____

Where do you most often find yourself looking for peace apart from Christ? Fill in the blanks.

I have been looking for peace in _____.

I have been looking for peace in _____.

I have been looking for peace in _____.

Now replace those words by writing this on the lines below: *I will find peace in Jesus.*

_____

_____

_____

I'm not going to lie. I'd prefer it if Jesus would have said, "I have told you these things so that in me you may have peace—because if you simply follow my instructions, life will be fun and easy and pain-free. Hooray!" Please tell me I'm not the only one. I would have liked to save my younger self (and my current self) from the heartbreak and uncertainty and fear that come from living in a fallen and broken world.

But even as I write this, I know my thinking is flawed. If life was absent of trouble, or if peace and perfection were within our reach, we wouldn't need a Savior. Jesus didn't come to teach us how to control life and avoid pain. He came to overcome the world and give us His peace on earth.

The peace of Jesus comes in His fierce with-ness. Do you know what I mean by that? No matter what happens, no matter what storm rages or what circumstances rock your world, Jesus will be right there with you. Even as Jesus prepared His disciples for His departure, He assured them of His steadfast commitment. "I will not leave you as orphans; I am coming to you" (John 14:18).

Read Deuteronomy 31:6–8; Isaiah 41:10; and Matthew 28:18–20.
What do these verses tell you about the reliability of God's presence?
How does this affect your sense of peace?

_____

_____

_____

_____

_____

Take a moment and think of a challenging situation or trial. Maybe it's an issue at work, a conflict with a close friend, or an inner struggle you have never even named. Hold it in your mind. Feel the tension it causes in your body. Let the mental and emotional weight you carry transfer to your physical body. Now add Jesus to your picture. Right in the middle of that family crisis or worrisome visit to the doctor, imagine Jesus is sitting beside you. No matter what happens next, He's not leaving.

Take a deep breath. Inhale the gift of His presence.

This is the peace of Jesus. Not that your circumstances will instantly change or that the road ahead will be free of painful potholes and disheartening detours, but that God the Son in the person of Jesus Christ and the Holy Spirit whom He sent *go with you*.

The peace of Jesus comes in His fierce with-ness. No matter what happens, no matter what storm rages or what circumstances rock your world, Jesus will be right there with you.

He has existed since before the foundation of the world, and He is the foundation of our present and our future. Paul explains it like this in Colossians 1:15–20:

> He is the image of the invisible God,
> the firstborn over all creation.
> For everything was created by him,
> in heaven and on earth,
> the visible and the invisible,
> whether thrones or dominions
> or rulers or authorities—
> all things have been created through him and for him.
> He is before all things,
> and by him all things hold together.
> He is also the head of the body, the church;
> he is the beginning, the firstborn from the dead,
> so that he might come to have
> first place in everything.
> For God was pleased to have
> all his fullness dwell in him,
> and through him to reconcile
> everything to himself,
> whether things on earth or things in heaven,
> by making peace
> through his blood, shed on the cross.

What does it mean that Jesus has overcome the world? It means death doesn't have the final say. It means Jesus's blood conquered the spiritual chaos caused by sin.

There is no peace without Jesus. Thank God we have Him.

Read Colossians 1:17. If Jesus holds all things together, that means you don't have to. How would trusting God to hold things together give you more peace today?

_____

_____

_____

_____

SCRIPTURE MEMORY MOMENT

Test yourself on John 14:27. Try to say it out loud and write it from memory. As we move into the next week of our study, hide these words in your heart and reflect on them often. Perhaps write John 14:27 on a sticky note and put it somewhere you'll see it every day.

A PRAYER FOR TODAY

JESUS, *I'm just really grateful. I'm grateful that trials and sorrow aren't the end of the story. Thank You that any trouble I face is temporary in view of the eternity I get to spend with You. And I know that anything I face today, You face it with me. I am not alone. Your presence is my peace. Make me ever mindful of the gift of Your Spirit. Keep teaching and guiding my heart. Amen.*

PEACE IS A POSTURE

The world offers plenty of formulas for peace, from self-care to incessant striving. Our culture preaches that contentment comes from having more and doing more, and that peace is found in numbing over and vegging out. But what if true satisfaction isn't found in something you can purchase or accomplish or in a way to escape? What if true peace is found in growing into the qualities of Jesus?

This week we're embarking on a journey of discovering how peace is a posture. The way we train our minds and spend our lives matters. Our attitude can be either a barrier to or a conduit of God's peace. Through our study, we'll explore several essential characteristics of people who experience the life-changing peace God offers. Characteristics like humility, stillness, trust, and contentment.

As we'll see in our opening story from (in)courage writer Anna E. Rendell, peace also comes through the posture of acceptance. Through the ups and downs of regular life and an intense season of transition, she knows that God is right there with her. As you read Anna's story, consider how your sense of peace ebbs and flows with your circumstances and how God might be reminding you to keep your mind fixed on Him.

A Story of Peace

Certain times in my life have been overcrowded with activities and commitments. Times when work has been demanding, family has been stressful, and the laundry piles have been intense. But two seasons in particular stand out to me as being full, overloaded, and too much, yet I felt peaceful during them.

Several years ago, my husband and I put our house up for sale for the second time in two years, and after months of cleaning and staging and spending a lot of time in our minivan during showings (three little kids don't exactly make open houses easy!), it finally sold. While we waited to move into the home we had purchased, our whole family of five (plus our dog) moved into my mom's townhome. We took over her hallway and spare bedroom, piling necessary belongings into the bathroom cabinets and cramming around her dining room table for family meals.

That autumn we lived with my sweet mom, many other events could have (perhaps even should have) made for a less-than-peaceful time. Life was just so much! On top of the added stress were all of the usual daily happenings. Laundry and dishes. Work meetings and packing lunches. Walking the dog and vacuuming. Brushing hair and cooking meals. Paying bills and finding missing socks. Regular life, which can be stressful in and of itself, marching on even amid the total chaos of living in such close quarters.

Yet underneath the outward mayhem . . . peace.

Even the weekend that two of my children took turns throwing up all night.

Even when we had to dive deep into our storage unit to find our winter coats.

Even on my kids' first day of preschool, seeing them off while I worked from the same small dining room table in my mom's home.

Through it all, I felt an inner peace I couldn't explain.

It honestly made no sense! Everything appeared to be an overwhelmed shambles . . . and yet, I experienced joy, contentment, and peace. Zero parts of my life looked like I'd pictured or even hoped they would. Yet when I look back on that upside-down season—even with an intentional effort *not* to wear the rose-colored glasses of hindsight—all I remember is happiness.

I think a part of me had settled into my circumstances like they were a big comfy chair, and I was sinking in to accept it all.

It's happened at other times in my life too—times when I fully expected the stress or unease to engulf my heart and instead peace flooded in.

The other season that stands out to me began the day I took my last pregnancy test and it was positive. Of all four of my children, that was the calmest I'd ever been taking that test. Pregnancy isn't usually a calm time for me but rather a time that includes fear due to unexplained infertility and loss. I've had two miscarriages, one on either side of my oldest son. Both were traumatic, painful, and took a long time to heal from. So for me, a positive pregnancy test brings both joy for what could be ahead and fear of that unknown.

But this test, the one that confirmed I was expecting my fourth child, was the most peace-filled of them all. I simply realized that I had missed my period. At the store, I nonchalantly tossed a pregnancy test onto the conveyor belt at checkout, right there among my groceries. When I got home, I took the test. And when my husband and I had a brief, quiet moment in the kitchen while our kids waited for us to bring dinner to the table, I calmly told him all about it.

What usually would have thrown me into a whirlwind of emotions, including fear and panic, became covered in simple peace. It was as though my heart had decided to be content whatever the circumstances, despite my painful past and jaggedly healed wounds. And the only explanation I could come up with was that God was at work in and through it all. Maybe God really did have a plan for me and my family. Maybe I really could trust His hand. Maybe, just maybe, no matter what happened, God would remain and that would be enough.

Maybe peace comes with acceptance, a lack of control, a hopeful contentment.

In each of those moments when peace replaced the usual chaos, I had accepted my circumstances. I knew Jesus walked with me, and even though hope felt far away, my heart felt peaceful. It was the best kind of strange, an unexplainable peace that surpassed understanding. God was teaching my heart to hold a posture of peace. How grateful I am for the depth of His kindness.

—ANNA E. RENDELL

When have you experienced the peace of Christ in difficult, unexpected, or unfavorable circumstances? Describe that moment or season.

_____

_____

_____

_____

Read Philippians 4:11–13. Whose strength did Paul rely on? What does this tell you about the key to being content in all circumstances?

_____

_____

_____

_____

Look up Romans 15:13. What does Paul say God will fill us with? What is required of us?

_____

_____

_____

_____

SCRIPTURE MEMORY MOMENT

This week's memory verse is Isaiah 26:3. Write out the verse in your journal (as printed here from the NLT or from your favorite translation). Throughout the week, commit these words to memory, asking God to create in you a heart of peace as you adopt a posture of peace.

> *You will keep in perfect peace*
>   *all who trust in you,*
>   *all whose thoughts are fixed on you!*

A PRAYER FOR TODAY

GOD, *thank You for infusing your peace into both hard seasons and ordinary days. Oh, how I need You. I need You to remind me that You are in control. I need You to help me surrender my present and my future circumstances to You. Lord, You are trustworthy. I know that! Help me to live every day from that reality and teach me to adopt a posture of peace and contentment. Thank You for guiding me on this journey of becoming more like Jesus. Amen.*

He says, "Be still, and know that I am God;
  I will be exalted among the nations,
  I will be exalted in the earth."

                      Psalm 46:10 NIV

Are you naturally inclined to be still, or is it a struggle? How does still-ness make you more aware of God's presence and peace?

_____

_____

_____

_____

As we talked about last week, Christ's birth was first announced to shepherds watching their flocks under a blanket of stars (Luke 2:13). Just think about that for a minute. The sky was suddenly filled with celestial beings breaking out in worship. Wow! First the heavenly host praised God. Then they foretold what was coming: peace.

But the angels aren't the only surprising characters in this story.

For centuries, the nation of Israel had been anxiously awaiting the promised Messiah. Jewish leaders and historians had predicted what the Messiah's arrival would look like, and they painted a picture of great pomp and circumstance. The Messiah was supposed to be a king, after all. A great ruler! The Lord of Lords! Surely His arrival would be heralded to only the most esteemed audience.

But that's not how the story unfolds. Instead of being announced to a royal court or prestigious religious leaders, the long-awaited Savior of the world was first revealed to a handful of lowly shepherds. These men who spent their days and nights in the fields were not elevated or celebrated. Their job was necessary but menial. In the world's eyes, a shepherd wasn't anyone special. A shepherd couldn't boast of an impressive education or cultural influence. Shepherds tended stinky sheep across a vast landscape. They were literally on the outskirts of society.

Yet they are the ones God chose to hear the angels proclaim, "Glory to God in the highest heaven, and peace on earth to people he favors."

Why do you think God chose to send His Son through the womb of a woman instead of in a blazing cloud or other majestic appearance? Why announce Jesus's arrival to shepherds instead of to kings?

_____

_____

_____

_____

Read the following verses and record the primary characteristic that is highlighted in all of them. Why do you think God desires this quality from His people?

Proverbs 16:19 _____

_____

Zephaniah 2:3 _____

_____

Matthew 5:5 _____

_____

1 Peter 5:5 _____

_____

_____

_____

_____

Consider this: the news of Jesus's arrival might have been lost in the noise of a grand palace or a large party. Kings and queens might have postured for better position instead of turning their full attention to God's holy message. But with their flocks settled in for the night, the shepherds had nothing to focus on but the vast sky and the twinkling stars.

It wasn't a mistake that the almighty God gave a grand show to a group of lowly shepherds the night Jesus was born. It was a built-in proclamation that Jesus came for *everyone*. That He bends low to elevate the lowly. That He shows Himself to the overlooked so that everyone would be seen. That His peace and presence are available to all.

How does someone know God? How does someone receive the good news of great joy that is for all people? We can find the answer in Psalm 46:10:

> Be still, and know that I am God;
>   I will be exalted among the nations,
>   I will be exalted in the earth. (NIV)

Interestingly, these peace-filled instructions to *be still and know* are in the context of a battle. Read all of Psalm 46 if you have time and notice how the psalmist uses war imagery to demonstrate that God's steadfast presence leads to victory.

The shepherds weren't in the middle of a physical battle that starry night, but humanity was in a spiritual battle. We still are.

The Christian Standard Bible translates Psalm 46:10 as "Stop fighting, and know that I am God."

Stop fighting. Stop striving. Stop worrying about yesterday or tomorrow or next year. Stop believing that you have control and that grasping for more of it will lead to more peace.

Friend, God is God and we are not. God is God and you are not. God is God and I am not. And because He knows we're slow and prideful and fearful human beings, our gentle and compassionate God tenderly invites us to be still and remember who He is.

Still your body and mind, still your need for control, still your expectations and careful planning, and *know that He is God.*

> **How are the qualities of humility and stillness countercultural? What fight do you need to surrender today so that you can be still and turn your focus to Jesus?**

The shepherds' ordinary circumstances placed them in a posture of stillness and humility. They weren't striving to change their situation or scheming for a way to be noticed. Most often, we are *not* in a natural

Stillness is a posture we have to intentionally choose.
Stillness acknowledges that God is trustworthy.
And it's a posture essential to our peace.

position of stillness. Like Anna shared in her opening story, regular life can be busy and chaotic. Add on seasons of transition, holidays, hardships, or anything out of the norm, and it's enough to make your head spin. A big move, a job change or promotion, a new baby, the loss of a relationship, injury or illness, betrayal, and political turmoil can all ratchet up the intensity of our lives a few more notches. When this happens, our pride seeks to protect us while nonstop movement—whether mental or physical—preoccupies and exhausts us.

Stillness is a posture we have to intentionally *choose*. Stillness acknowledges that God is trustworthy. And it's a posture essential to our peace. King David, who was at one time a shepherd, records in Psalm 62:1, "I am at rest in God alone; my salvation comes from him."

I would never have the conscious thought that my salvation comes from *me*. I know it comes from God. I know I can't earn His grace and forgiveness. Yet there have been times when I have lived like I believed otherwise. Times I have strived to be good enough, moral enough, successful enough to guarantee my own security—my own peace. When we fall into these patterns, we let pride take root in our lives. But we cannot rest in God when we are trusting in ourselves.

Humble yourself today, sister. Take a deep breath and still your soul. Look up. You may not see the heavens open to a choir of angels, but surely you will see the fingerprints of the one who hung each star and formed each cloud and planned in advance a way for you to know Him and experience His peace.

Read Psalm 62. While you won't find the word *peace* in these lines, what do you learn about the character of God? How does who He is lead you to peace?

_____

_____

_____

_____

SCRIPTURE MEMORY MOMENT

Write out Isaiah 26:3. How will you fix your thoughts on God this week? Now text this verse to a friend who might be encouraged by it. Invite her to memorize it with you!

A PRAYER FOR TODAY

JESUS, *thank You for coming to earth in the most surprising way to the most surprising group of people in order to demonstrate Your love for all people—especially those who are often overlooked. Thank You that I don't have to perform or strive for the peace You offer. I need only be still. Yet sometimes that's really hard to do. Grow me in humility and create in me a heart of peace. I love You and I trust You. Amen.*

DAY 3

I know what it is to be in need, and I know what it is to have plenty. I have learned the secret of being content in any and every situation, whether well fed or hungry, whether living in plenty or in want. I can do all this through him who gives me strength.

Philippians 4:12–13 NIV

Have you experienced a time in your life when you felt truly content? What was the source of your inner settledness or satisfaction?

_____

_____

_____

_____

Do you ever hear someone talk about peace and then look at their life and think, *Well yeah, it's easy for you to be content! Look at how perfect and easy your life is!* Meanwhile, peace in your own life feels crowded out by trial after trial, struggle after struggle. How can you be content when the basement floods, the baby won't sleep through the night, the teenager won't obey curfew, the budget's too tight, loneliness is a constant companion, and you hurt your hip in your sleep? (Is it just me?)

It's easy to associate peace and contentment with pleasant circumstances. Surely that's the message our culture preaches. Just buy that new skincare product, organize your closet, put your kid in that program, throw the perfect party, read the self-help book, and earn that promotion. Ta-da! *Then* you will be content with your life. And yet . . . I don't know anyone who has done *all the things* and didn't wind up just creating another list of must-haves and must-dos.

Even if we're not swayed by material things, we do this with spiritual matters. Just help with that ministry and attend that retreat, check off your quiet time box, make your donation, and pray before every meal. Surely those good things will lead to the peace we long for, right?

Looking for contentment by doing good things *for* Jesus won't replace the peace found *in* Jesus.

The apostle Paul writes, "I can do all this through him who gives me strength." Too often Christians apply this verse to mean "I can do anything I want by the power of God." While it's true that God does empower His people to do a multitude of things, in the context of Philippians 4, Paul isn't talking about things like running a marathon, starting a business, or even serving the poor. He's talking about how to live from a posture of contentment. How to find an inner stability, serenity, and satisfaction that don't hinge on our present situation.

Whether he had a full belly or felt hunger pangs, as a free man or in prison chains, Paul learned that peace isn't found in the presence of abundance or the absence of hardship. Peace is the quiet strength provided by Jesus.

Read Philippians 4:12–13 again. What have you learned about contentment? When have you experienced Christ's strength in this way, or when have you witnessed it at work in someone else?

_____

_____

_____

_____

Read 1 Timothy 6:6–12. How has a desire for money caused roots of discontentment in your life? What does this passage say we ought to pursue?

_____

_____

_____

_____

Is money bad? No. Is having a pantry stocked with food bad? No. Having a surplus or living paycheck to paycheck doesn't make you a better or worse Christian. In fact, Paul's teaching on contentment is not about our circumstances. Learning to be content in *any situation* tells us that peace is found apart from the external.

To understand this better, let's back up a bit to Philippians 3 and read more about the man who claimed this life of contentment. Here's how Paul describes his background:

> For we who worship by the Spirit of God are the ones who are truly circumcised. We rely on what Christ Jesus has done for us. We put no confidence in human effort, though I could have confidence in my own effort if anyone could. Indeed, if others have reason for confidence in their own efforts, I have even more!
>
> I was circumcised when I was eight days old. I am a pure-blooded citizen of Israel and a member of the tribe of Benjamin—a real Hebrew if there ever was one! I was a member of the Pharisees, who demand the strictest obedience to the Jewish law. I was so zealous that I harshly persecuted the church. And as for righteousness, I obeyed the law without fault. (vv. 3–6 NLT)

Basically, Paul is saying, "I was a super-awesome-letter-of-the-law-perfect Jew who checked every box and earned every religious gold star. If anyone should be pleased with their life and accomplishments, it should be me!"

No doubt Paul's friends and fellow religious leaders had looked at him and thought, *Man, that guy has it together. He's living the good life. What more could he need or want?*

But this is not the set of circumstances that led Paul to a life of peace and contentment.

> **Continue reading Philippians 3:7–9. How does Jesus change Paul's perspective on earthly pursuits? What are you holding on to or striving for today, hoping that it will give you the contentment you long for?**

After Paul experienced a dramatic conversion (see Acts 9) and started preaching the good news of Jesus instead of persecuting those who did, his life was filled with hardship . . . and peace. Paul was beaten, abandoned, and imprisoned. He battled sickness and loneliness. He begged God to remove a "thorn in the flesh," which God refused to do. "Each time he said, 'My grace is all you need. My power works best in weakness.' So now I am glad to boast about my weaknesses, so that the power of Christ can work through me" (2 Cor. 12:9 NLT).

This is the way Paul learned to be content in every situation. This is the way we can learn to be content in every situation. Paul's source of peace wasn't in his own accolades but in the atoning forgiveness of Jesus. His peace wasn't in his own efforts but in the effective grace of

Jesus. Paul no longer identified himself by his pedigree and prestige because his true identity was in Jesus.

Paul took on a posture of contentment, which enabled him to experience the life-changing peace of Jesus. In our opening story on day 1, Anna wasn't in jail or worried about being flogged or wondering where she was going to preach next. Our circumstances don't have to be extreme for us to need God's peace.

On a regular Tuesday when you run out of laundry detergent. On a Saturday night when you get a phone call that makes your heart sink. When you're treated unfairly, when you get overlooked, when your security net falls through, when a door slams in your face—every moment of every day you have a choice to make. Are you going to look for happiness in what's happening around you? Or are you going to look for strength and peace from the one who is in you?

Choose well today, friend.

> Read Romans 8:6 along with this week's memory verse from Isaiah 26:3. How does what we think about affect our peace and contentment? Who or what is leading your thoughts today?

SCRIPTURE MEMORY MOMENT

Write out Isaiah 26:3 and think about an area of your life God is asking you to trust Him with more fully.

A PRAYER FOR TODAY

DEAR GOD, *I so desperately want to learn the secret of being content. Not just learn it in my head as a lesson I can regurgitate but learn it in my soul so that it stays with me and I can live it out no matter what tomorrow holds. Thank You for offering me Your strength in my weakness, Your peace in my hard and ordinary circumstances. I want more of You. Help me this week to live from a posture of dependency on You. I trust You and I love You. Amen.*

DAY 4

What has the biggest influence on your attitude each day?

_____

_____

_____

_____

Your baby is teething and kept waking up at all hours of the night. A rude driver cut you off on your morning commute. Your roommate left her dishes on the kitchen counter—*again.*

Ugh. Can you feel the tension crawling up your neck?

Or maybe you woke up to a perfect hair day. Your kind neighbor brought in your trash cans. Your kids didn't fight on the way to school, and the predicted storm instead gave way to clear blue skies.

Hooray! What a glorious day!

It sure is easy to let things that are beyond our control—whether bad or good—dictate our attitude. I see this in my kids too. If they get to play the video game of their choice—happy campers. If I ask them to take a family walk or bring in the trash cans—grumpy complainers. While I desire for (and expect) my children to choose a grateful and cheerful manner whether they get what they want or not, I have to admit I don't always follow my own standards.

But what does the Bible have to say about our attitude? In a nutshell, it says we should take a cue from Jesus. Listen again to the instruction of the apostle Paul from his letter to the Philippians: "Do nothing out of selfish ambition or conceit, but in humility consider others as more important than yourselves. Everyone should look not to his own interests, but rather to the interests of others" (2:3–4).

There's that word *humility* again. It means turning away from self-focus to other-focus, having a posture that chooses to serve instead of strive, remembering that God is in control and we are not. These instructions lead us to the big takeaway: "Adopt the same attitude as that of Christ Jesus" (v. 5).

Continue reading Philippians 2:6–11. Based on this passage, how would you describe Jesus's attitude? What qualities does Paul say we should emulate?

_____

_____

_____

_____

Now read Philippians 2:5–8 again. Really think about what Jesus, the Son of God, did in coming to earth and dying on the cross. How do His service and sacrifice reframe your attitude or perspective today?

_____

_____

When I was younger in my faith, I remember reading Paul's instructions and thinking it was kind of ridiculous. I mean, Jesus is *Jesus*. The Savior. God in human flesh. Sacrifice and obedience must come easy for Him, right? How can God expect imperfect us to have the same attitude as perfect Jesus?

While I understand where my younger self was coming from, in truth it was a cop-out. I didn't want to put others first. It felt like a lot of pressure to try living up to Jesus's standards. The bar was too high! How could any of us possibly reach it?

If you find your mind wandering down this same lane of thinking, it's time for a full stop. Paul's instructions to adopt a Christlike posture are not a prescription for religious performance but an invitation to spiritual freedom, to eternal peace in Jesus rather than temporary pleasure in ourselves.

Jesus Himself said, "So if the Son sets you free, you really will be free" (John 8:36). We don't have to perfectly follow an elaborate set of rules or offer animal sacrifices on an altar to be made right with God. We don't have to earn our salvation or be a really good person for God to love us. "For you are saved by grace through faith, and this is not from yourselves; it is God's gift—not from works, so that no one can boast" (Eph. 2:8–9).

We will beat this drum as loud and as long and as often as we need to! Nothing about the peace of Jesus is wrapped up in our performance.

Nothing about the peace of Jesus is wrapped up in our performance.

Yet God does invite us to *partner* with Him. We'll talk more about this in week 6 when we address how peace is our purpose. But this truth is an applicable reminder for us today. Scripture lays out instructions and encouragement that are for our benefit.

If we want to experience the peace Jesus came to give, it only makes sense that we would be ready to follow His lead.

Do you struggle with living like you have to earn God's love and favor, or even His peace? What truth do you need to cling to and rehearse today?

So what does adopting the same attitude as Jesus look like practically? Paul's teaching in Philippians 2 goes on to unpack this: "Do everything without grumbling and arguing, so that you may be blameless and pure, children of God who are faultless in a crooked and perverted genera-tion, among whom you shine like stars in the world, by holding firm to the word of life" (vv. 14–16).

Hold firm to the word of *life*. That's the goal, friend! Jesus said it Him-self: "I have come so that they may have life and have it in abundance" (John 10:10). How do we get this abundant life? Follow God's Word and Christ's example. Don't grumble or complain. Be different from this dark world so you will shine brightly. In this way, the world will know whose you are!

I love the way The Message translates Paul's instructions from Philippians 2:

> Do everything readily and cheerfully—no bickering, no second-guessing allowed! Go out into the world uncorrupted, a breath of fresh air in this squalid and polluted society. Provide people with a glimpse of good living and of the living God. (vv. 14–16)

I'll confess, I often want my children to stop bickering and start loving each other cheerfully because it makes life easier on *me*. But make no mistake, God's motive is not selfish. God doesn't want to keep us in line so life is better for Him. He wants us to heed His Word and pattern our lives after Jesus so life is better for us! And in the process, others will see the difference it makes in our lives and want to know Jesus, the life-giving Prince of Peace, too.

Assess your attitude on an average day—not your worst and not your best. How does your usual posture compare to Jesus's example? What do you need to adjust to reflect more of your Savior's heart?

_____

_____

_____

SCRIPTURE MEMORY MOMENT

Write out Isaiah 26:3 and consider how keeping your mind dependent on God affects your attitude. If you have time, write the verse three more times in your journal.

A PRAYER FOR TODAY

JESUS, *I want to be more like You. Help me adopt Your attitude of humility. Help me take on Your posture of servant-heartedness. I confess I'm often prone to grumble and complain. Help me exchange my irritability for Your peace. May Your light shine through me. I'm Yours. Thank You for being my Savior and Guide. Amen.*

DAY 5

Trust in the Lᴏʀᴅ with all your heart;
    do not depend on your own understanding.
Seek his will in all you do,
    and he will show you which path to take.
                              Proverbs 3:5-6 NLT

When has trusting God led to peace in your life?

_____

_____

_____

_____

Peace always sounds like such a pleasant quality or experience, doesn't it? The tranquil sound of a babbling brook. The gentle spirit of a sweet friend. A quiet afternoon with the company of a good book. On the surface, peace is the absence of anything unpleasant.

But a peaceful environment is not the same as a peaceful soul.

We see this distinction clearly in Anna's story from day 1. With her history of infertility and miscarriage, seeing those double pink lines on the pregnancy test normally would have sent Anna into an emotional

68

tailspin of fear and worry. But this time something was different. This time her heart was at peace because her trust was in Jesus.

We've been talking about how peace is a posture, and a key characteristic of that posture is surrender. (I know the "s" word can be scary. Don't tune out! Lean in, friend. This is life-changing!)

We cannot experience the peace of Jesus if we're not willing to give our whole lives—what we think about, our attitude, and the outcome of our circumstances—to Him. All week we've been memorizing Isaiah 26:3: "You will keep in perfect peace all who trust in you, all whose thoughts are fixed on you!" Ultimately, the posture of peace comes down to a posture of trust.

> Read Genesis 3:1–7. (If you're familiar with this story, try to read it with fresh eyes.) What led Eve and Adam to choose to eat the forbidden fruit? What was the underlying issue they faced?

We cannot experience the peace of Jesus if we're not willing to give our whole lives—what we think about, our attitude, and the outcome of our circumstances—to Him.

When have you ignored what Scripture teaches or what you felt the Holy Spirit was leading you to do for the sake of going after what seemed better in your own eyes?

_____

_____

_____

_____

When Eve took a bite of that tantalizing fruit, she wasn't just breaking a rule, like a kid who sneaks a snack before dinner when their parent told them to wait. No, this was about way more than spoiling their appetites. This was about trusting God's word and trusting His heart. Essentially, the serpent's slick question made the woman and man second-guess God's intention toward them. Did He really have their best interests in mind? Or was He holding out on them?

Have you ever secretly wondered the same thing? When life goes sideways, do you question whether God is still in control? If He asks you to take the long way around when you clearly see a shortcut right in front of you, do you wonder if His way is really best? These are normal thoughts and feelings. I know I've had them.

But choosing a life with Jesus means acknowledging that _He_ is God and we are not.

Proverbs 3:5–6 says it clearly:

> Trust in the Lord with all your heart;
>   do not depend on your own understanding.
> Seek his will in all you do,
>   and he will show you which path to take. (NLT)

Adam and Eve chose to depend on their own understanding. *That fruit looks delicious. If I eat it, maybe I'll become like God. That would be awesome.* BITE. And sin enters the world. Oops!

Of course, this is an oversimplified summary, but boiling it down like this makes the first man and woman's error pretty obvious. They didn't trust in God with all their heart. In that moment, they decided instead to trust the voice of another along with their own desires.

> **Look up Proverbs 3:5–6 in three or four translations using a Bible app on a smartphone or by going to Biblegateway.com. Make a note of what words are used for "depend" and "seek his will." How does each word choice enhance your understanding of what this passage is warning you against and calling you to?**

In order to adopt a posture of trust, we must resolve in our hearts and minds that God is trustworthy. I know this might feel like we're getting off-track from our discussion of peace and surrender, but hang in there with me. This is important. While we can't dissect God's track record and every aspect of His character in a single lesson, here are three important tools that will help us determine God is trustworthy:

1. **Read** the story of God's people through Scripture and look for what He says about Himself.
2. **Remember** what God has done in your own life.
3. **Rehearse** His faithfulness often.

God rescued the Israelites out of slavery in Egypt, parted the Red Sea for them, led them through the wilderness and eventually into the promised land, and demonstrated His love, care, and provision for them. Did every part of the journey make sense in their eyes? Not by a long shot. But their doubts didn't change God's plan. Their wondering and wandering didn't change the goodness and trustworthiness of His path.

The same is true for us today.

If you look for evidence that God is worthy of your trust, you will find it. If you seek His will in your work life and marriage, in your friendships and motherhood, in who you choose to date and where you serve and what vacation you take and how you pay rent, He *will* lead you. And when you choose to follow Jesus, His peace will be your companion.

> Read Psalm 9:10. Where are you tempted to lean on your own understanding? How can you seek God and His will in that area of your life?

SCRIPTURE MEMORY MOMENT

Test yourself on Isaiah 26:3. Try to say it out loud and write it from memory. As we move into the next week of our study, hide these words in your heart and reflect on them often. Perhaps write Isaiah 26:3 on a sticky note and put it somewhere you'll see it every day.

A PRAYER FOR TODAY

LORD JESUS, *I trust in You. Not like a gumball machine, putting in my quarter of trust so I get the treat of Your peace. I entrust my life to You. I believe You are God and that Your ways are loving and good. I pray Paul's words from Romans 15:13 and ask that You would honor them in my life today: May the God of hope fill me with all joy and peace as I trust in Him, so that I may overflow with hope by the power of the Holy Spirit. Amen.*

PEACE IS A PROMISE

Experiencing the peace of God means trusting God and following Him—no matter what. If words like *obedience* and *surrender* make you flinch, it's time to reexamine the peace and freedom God offers when we let Him lead.

But it's that *no matter what* part that gets sticky, right? In today's lesson, we'll discover how peace is a promise that transcends our circumstances. Because while our bank account balance may fluctuate, our favor with influential leaders may falter, and our health may fail, God never changes. His peace doesn't flicker or fade. He is reliable, steadfast, and sure. Keep this in mind as you read today's opening story from (in)courage writer Jen Schmidt. Consider how life's unexpected blessings and blows have led you to cling to His promises all the more.

A Story of Peace

The long walk down our country gravel drive to our mailbox seemed different on this day. For years, it had been blissfully routine. I'd take a few minutes out of my day to breathe deeply and enjoy nature. But for weeks now, this walk had been filled with trepidation. Hesitantly opening the box, I wondered if today was my bad news day. It was.

I entered the house with the stark reality that we could not pay critical bills and notice was served. I felt suffocated. I tried to slow my breathing to right myself.

A failing business, the stock market crash, our loan offering to help a friend in need, and then unemployment all resulted in devastating financial times.

Pulling at my legs, my little ones gathered around me wondering what was wrong. I'm not a crier, so they knew it was bad. It all felt so unfair. We hadn't spent foolishly. In fact, we were trying to help others, but everything had spun out of our control.

With my head down and babies drawn near, I clearly heard God remind me, "Peace I leave with you. My peace I give to you. I do not give to you as the world gives. Don't let your heart be troubled or fearful" (John 14:27).

I was tempted to yell back, "Lord, how about 'Solid employment I leave with you. Children who make wise choices I give to you. Marital bliss I promise you'?" But God knew that my wants and desires were not what was needed.

Jesus gives His disciples this promise of His peace on their last night together. Knowing He is about to depart from earth, He doesn't teach a new kind of gospel but rather gives His closest friends—and all of us—the gift of remembering that we already have everything we need in Him.

Christ's declaration didn't solve my immediate financial dilemma. Paying for groceries was still a challenge. My soul was worn-out, and I wrestled with worry. But I wrote John 14:27 on my mirror, committed it to memory, and invited our children into the journey of receiving Jesus's peace.

So when our third-grade son reiterated his lesson from the book of Esther later that week, it was like the Lord Himself speaking words of comfort over me.

"Mom, Esther didn't know what was going to happen to her either, but she stepped out in faith for such a time as this."

"Yes, she did, bud."

The Lord used our son to remind me of that guaranteed promise: peace. An overwhelming, can't-explain-the-depth-amid-despair kind of peace. That's what Jesus left for us.

Peace when unemployment looms once again. Peace while we're on our knees for wayward children. Peace when devastation hits those we love. Peace is our promise, and He is our Promise Keeper.

And just in case I hadn't learned this crucial lesson after that experience, I got a refresher course about ten years later.

Fast-forward to when my husband's employer announced their company had been bought out and they'd be closing his department. With hindsight and wisdom forged through intense difficulties, I was able to remember that Jesus is my constant source for peace.

I declared His promise. My Helper, the Holy Spirit, whom the Father sent, reminded me of all that He had taught me and said to me over the years of following Him, of trusting Him, of claiming His truth on behalf of our future (John 14:26).

So when the fear and doubt crept subtly into the crevices of my heart once again as one month of unemployment became two, and two became twelve, I begged God to not let me forget. To remind me to rest in His reassurance that circumstances do not determine my peace. That the world cannot take it away. That I can choose to cling to Jesus, our source of peace.

Fast-forward again. They say something about the third time, right?

Six months before COVID-19 quarantined us, an old house nearby that had stood empty for a decade was listed for sale below tax value. Creating a hospitality house close to our own home had been a ministry dream I'd envisioned for years. This was an answer to decades of prayers. Not only could I host welcoming weekends for women, but I'd also have the ability to offer rooms for those in need of respite.

For more than twenty years I had learned the hard lessons. I had saved. I had prayed. I had made a budget. So of course, I reasoned, *this* would be God's will, and my dream of furthering the gospel through strategic hospitality would finally be realized.

We put in an offer we could afford based on our employment. I included a heartfelt letter explaining the ways this hospitality house would impact the area. While my pockets weren't deep, my heart was huge, so I waited for my Hallmark ending. It didn't come.

I grieved the "what could have been" plans I'd already made as disappointment loomed, but I remembered what Jesus promised. His timing is intricately woven into His best plans for my life. I know that. He continues to reveal it through a lifetime of following Him, but sometimes I'm a slow learner.

When all our kids came home during the early shelter-in-place order, one dinner discussion centered around the reality that after dreaming for decades about building our hospitality house, it may never happen. And you know what I felt? Total peace. We pondered the gift of listening and waiting through long seasons of difficult obedience. COVID cost many of us employment, including me. If we had bought that historic house the year before, it could have culminated in financial disaster. We could not have foreseen a worldwide pandemic, and yet God protected us. What a gift.

Over dessert, I looked around our home and saw air mattresses propped everywhere, with extra chairs pulled around the table to make room for our single friends who had no place to go.

"Guys, this home, this packed table, this welcoming space that He's called us to for this exact season—this is our hospitality house. I am living my dream."

Peace.

—JEN SCHMIDT

Have you ever watched a long-held dream deflate or disappear, or had a deep desire go unmet? How did God's peace meet you in that difficult place?

_____

_____

_____

_____

In week 1, we memorized John 14:27. How has this promise impacted your outlook or affected your faith?

_____

_____

_____

_____

Read all of John 14, remembering that this was part of Jesus's last words to His disciples. What other promises does Jesus give?

_____

_____

_____

_____

SCRIPTURE MEMORY MOMENT

This week's memory verse is 2 Thessalonians 3:16. Write out the verse in your journal (as printed here from the CSB or from your favorite translation). Throughout the week, commit these words to memory, asking God to create in you a heart of peace as you remember His promises.

May the Lord of peace himself give you peace always in every way. The Lord be with all of you.

A PRAYER FOR TODAY

JESUS, *thank You for being my source of peace. When the rug gets pulled out from under me, when dreams slip through my fingers, it's so easy to forget that Your peace hasn't changed. You are with me at all times, in all situations. Thank You. Create in me a heart of steadfast, lasting peace this week. Your peace! More of You and less of me, Jesus. Amen.*

They do not fear bad news;
they confidently trust the LORD to care for them.

Psalm 112:7 NLT

When have you been afraid of bad news? How did you get through that time of uncertainty?

_____

_____

_____

_____

On that long walk down her gravel driveway, Jen felt a sense of impending doom. Haven't we all been there? When you're afraid to answer the phone because the doctor might be calling with the test results. Or you're nervous to check your email because there might be a scathing reply from that person who has hurt you too many times to count. It's easy to fear turning on the news or scrolling Facebook. Will you learn about another school shooting, another racially motivated murder, another fallen church leader?

What a beautiful example Jen gives us that, in her season of wrestling through unemployment and uncertainty, she clung to the very promise we started this Bible study with: "Peace I leave with you. My peace I give to you. I do not give to you as the world gives. Don't let your heart be troubled or fearful" (John 14:27 NLT).

We're quick to grab for those first few words: "Peace I leave with you." Then Jesus reiterates it: "My peace I give to you." Our hearts cry out, *Yes! That's what I want! How do I get it?*

Jesus is the source of peace, but we have to partner with Him in order to receive the gift He offers.

"Don't let your hearts be troubled or fearful." *Do not let.* There it is. The reality that we have a choice. We can allow fear of the present or the future to overwhelm us, *or* we can cling to and claim the peace Jesus has promised.

> **Read the following passages and describe the relationship between our fear and God's character. Who is He? What does He ask us to do?**
>
> Psalm 112:7 _____
>
> _____
>
> Isaiah 41:10 _____
>
> _____
>
> 1 Peter 5:6–7 _____
>
> _____

> **In what area of your life do you need to give your fears and anxieties to God? Write out a short prayer surrendering your fears and acknowledging the promise of God's presence and care.**
>
> _____
>
> _____
>
> _____
>
> _____

> **The peace of God gives us power to do what we could never do on our own.**

One mark of someone who has a heart of peace from the Lord is that they are willing and able to follow God in the face of frightening circumstances.

In the opening story this week, Jen's son reminded her about the account of Queen Esther, who risked her life to save the Jews from annihilation. Reading the whole harrowing story in the book of Esther would definitely be worth your time. But listen carefully to the warning and promise Esther received from her cousin Mordecai:

> Don't think for a moment that because you're in the palace you will escape when all other Jews are killed. If you keep quiet at a time like this, deliverance and relief for the Jews will arise from some other place, but you and your relatives will die. Who knows if perhaps you were made queen for just such a time as this? (Esther 4:13–14 NLT)

Mordecai was clinging to God's promise to deliver His people. Esther had to decide: Would she also trust in God's protection and partner with Him, or would she run, hide, and forsake her God? Esther chose to believe that her unexpected position as queen of Persia was not by mistake but for such a time as this. Indeed, Esther used her circumstances to skillfully shine a light on Haman's evil plot and advocate on behalf of her people.

This is the thing about the peace of God: it gives us power to do what we could never do on our own.

Another Old Testament story that illustrates this truth comes from the book of Daniel. Nebuchadnezzar, king of Babylon, erects a ninety-foot gold statue of himself and commands everyone to bow down in worship to the statue every time they hear music being played. The dramatic plot thickens when Shadrach, Meshach, and Abednego, three Jewish men who serve Nebuchadnezzar as province managers, refuse to bow down to the golden sculpture.

Here's the scene when the men are brought before the king and he confronts them:

> Shadrach, Meshach, and Abednego, is it true that you don't serve my gods or worship the gold statue I have set up? Now if you're ready, when you hear the sound of the horn, flute, zither, lyre, harp, drum, and every kind of music, fall down and worship the statue I made. But if you don't worship it, you will immediately be thrown into a furnace of blazing fire—and who is the god who can rescue you from my power? (Dan. 3:14–15).

Can you put yourself in these guys' shoes for a minute? They are faced with a seemingly impossible decision. Abandon their faith and defy God, who clearly commanded them not to worship any other god or idol (Exod. 20:3–6), *or* be burned alive. If I were in that position, I imagine I might wet my pants or faint from fear. I might fall to my knees and beg the king to reconsider. I'd probably start devising a way to run and hide, or even lie my way out of the situation.

But that's not at all how these three friends responded.

> Shadrach, Meshach, and Abednego replied to the king, "Nebuchadnezzar, we don't need to give you an answer to this question. If the God we serve exists, then he can rescue us from the furnace of blazing fire, and he can rescue us from the power of you, the king. But even if he does not rescue us, we want you as king to know that we will not serve your gods or worship the gold statue you set up." (Dan. 3:16–18)

Wow.

What stands out to you about Shadrach, Meshach, and Abednego's response? Though the above verses don't use the words *peace* or *promise*, how do you see the threads of those ideas in this story?

_____

_____

_____

_____

God can rescue us, but even if he does not . . .

This, friend, is the power of peace.

We don't keep our hearts from being troubled because God promises that bad things will never happen. We've already talked about Jesus's clear and honest words on this: "In this world you will have trouble" (John 16:33). But His peace goes before us and is with us, and He has overcome the world! So no matter what happens here on earth, today or tomorrow or next year, our future is sealed! Does the degree of peace in your life show that you believe it?

So what happens after Shadrach, Meshach, and Abednego's bold refusal to worship Nebuchadnezzar's statue? In a nutshell, Nebuchadnezzar gets really, *really* mad. He commands the three men be tied up and the furnace be turned up seven times hotter than normal. It was so hot, in fact, that the soldiers who carry the prisoners to the edge of the furnace are themselves consumed by the flames and die! Then Shadrach, Meshach, and Abednego fall into the blazing fire.

And God meets them there.

When the king looks down into the furnace, he sees the three men walking around, unharmed, accompanied by a fourth person whom Nebuchadnezzar describes as "a son of the gods." At this, the king commands Shadrach, Meshach, and Abednego to come out of the furnace.

When they do, not a single hair on their heads is singed and not even a thread of their clothes smells like smoke.

And the king, who at first threatened to execute anyone who wouldn't worship him, turns in worship to the only one who deserves it:

> Nebuchadnezzar exclaimed, "Praise to the God of Shadrach, Meshach, and Abednego! He sent his angel and rescued his servants who trusted in him. They violated the king's command and risked their lives rather than serve or worship any god except their own God." (Dan. 3:28)

Like a flame leaping in the air, those words sear my heart: *his servants who trusted in him.*

Whatever is happening in your life today, you can have peace knowing God is in control. Your life is not dictated by an economic recession or a wicked king. God's goodness cannot be thwarted by a hurricane or hurt feelings. Your life isn't at the mercy of a layoff or leukemia or a loved one who chooses to stop loving you. Only Jesus can be your never-changing peace.

That's His promise to you.

Read Isaiah 43:2 and write it out in your own words, making it personal to you and the trials you are going through.

SCRIPTURE MEMORY MOMENT

Write out 2 Thessalonians 3:16. How has God been with you? Now text this verse to a friend who might be encouraged by it. Invite her to memorize it with you!

A PRAYER FOR TODAY

GOD, *thank You for promising to always be with me no matter what fire or storm I face. I trust You. Continue to teach me how to choose Your peace over my own fear. This week help me cling to Your promises instead of my own anxieties. You are powerful and good. I believe that—even when I still have to endure hard things. Thank You that I don't bear them alone. Amen.*

DAY 3

But the Holy Spirit produces this kind of fruit in our lives: love, joy, peace, patience, kindness, goodness, faithfulness, gentleness, and self-control. There is no law against these things!

Galatians 5:22–23 NLT

What's your honest reaction when you read about the fruit of the Spirit? Perhaps you feel excited, defeated, hopeful, or skeptical. Why might you feel that way?

_____

_____

_____

_____

We're going to start today by laying our cards on the table, so to speak. No hiding or holding back, okay? I'll go first.

Sometimes when I think about the fruit of the Spirit, it feels like a spiritual laundry list I'll never be able to conquer or live up to. On a good day, I might be able to manage being patient with my loud kids, loving to my husband, and faithful in the work God has called me to. But then I complain about chores instead of doing them with joy, an unkind word slips out of my mouth, and my prayer life and sugar addiction reveal a far cry from self-control.

I want to be a godly woman and I want a heart of peace, but sometimes it just seems impossible. Do you ever feel that way?

Whether you've grown up in the church and walked with Jesus for decades or you're just discovering what it means to know Christ, we can all have subtle lies take root in our hearts in the form of twisted truths. Things like . . .

No matter how hard you try, you'll never be a good Christian.

You'll always fall short of what the Bible commands.

You're not strong enough or disciplined enough to ever really grow or change.

Friend, the reason lies like these are so powerful is that they are bathed in partial truth. We will never be good—apart from Jesus. We will always fall short of what the Bible commands—without God's strength. And we won't be strong enough or disciplined enough for lasting change—unless the Spirit is working through us.

Our culture trains us to zero in on self. We ask, "What can *I* do?" But we must look at the whole picture! And whether we see Him or not, that whole picture always includes God.

If we want God to create in us a heart of peace, we must recognize, celebrate, and surrender to the truth that *God* is the *creator*. God the Father, God the Son, and God the Spirit are the molders, masters, and heart-shapers.

That's why Paul writes in Galatians about the fruit of the *Spirit* rather than the fruit of *self*! He knows that these amazing qualities—love, joy, peace, patience, kindness, goodness, faithfulness, gentleness, and self-control—are the result of being grafted to the Holy Spirit and producing *His* fruit.

What lies have taken root in your heart? List at least one here, and then write out the contrasting truth that includes the reality of God's power or presence.

_____

_____

_____

_____

Read John 14:15–27, paying special attention to verses 16 and 26. Why did Jesus ask the Father to send the Holy Spirit? What is the Spirit supposed to do?

_____

_____

_____

_____

Do you ever feel alone? Ever feel like you're hanging on in life by an unraveling thread, winging it and wishing you knew whether to go right or take a hard left? "And I will ask the Father, and he will give you another Counselor to be with you forever" (John 14:16).

Do you struggle with forgetfulness? Can't remember where you put your keys or what exactly was in that recipe or why you keep struggling with that same spiritual lesson? "But the Counselor, the Holy Spirit, whom the Father will send in my name, will teach you all things and remind you of everything I have told you" (John 14:26).

Jesus knew that His best friends were going to feel alone and adrift without Him. Jesus wasn't going to let His disciples fall apart and flail. He didn't want them to hustle and strive to the point of becoming a stressed-out mess all in the name of trying to do right by Jesus. He knew they needed more guidance. They needed a constant companion, supporter, encourager, and truth-reminder. The Holy Spirit is God's gift to Jesus's friends.

And the great news is that we are Jesus's friends too.

Read John 16:7–8. What role of the Holy Spirit is described here?

_____

_____

_____

_____

In a study about peace, it would be nice if we didn't have to bring up uncomfortable topics like sin and judgment. I'd rather turn up the tranquil spa music and talk about green meadows and peace like a river. But the truth is peace exists as one side of a dichotomy. War and peace. Sin and atonement. Brokenness and redemption. Peace is powerful because it stands in opposition to a toxic and terminal alternative.

Our souls desperately crave peace because without it—without Jesus—we're in perpetual turmoil. Sin and self entangle us. Without Jesus, unemployment and comparison can make us spiral into a cycle of just-try-harder. Without Jesus, broken relationships, battered reputations, and hidden addictions can turn up the dial of doubt and anxiety.

Our souls desperately crave peace because without it— without Jesus—we're in perpetual turmoil.

We need the Spirit to convict, save, and empower us! We need the peace of Jesus.

> When God our Savior revealed his kindness and love, he saved us, not because of the righteous things we had done, but because of his mercy. He washed away our sins, giving us a new birth and new life through the Holy Spirit. He generously poured out the Spirit upon us through Jesus Christ our Savior. Because of his grace he made us right in his sight and gave us confidence that we will inherit eternal life. (Titus 3:4–7 NLT)

Generously poured out the Spirit upon us. Do you see the gift? God didn't give us barely enough of Himself so we could just scrape by on righteousness. He didn't reserve the Holy Spirit as part of a bonus structure for "super Christians." No, He offered the Spirit lavishly—and that Spirit produces fruit in our lives that includes the peace we crave.

The power of peace is abundantly available to you today. First, for the forgiveness of your sins. Then, as the overflow of your fellowship and partnership with the Holy Spirit.

Following his famous list of spiritual fruit in Galatians 5:22–23, Paul gives this encouragement: "If we live by the Spirit, let us also keep in step with the Spirit" (v. 25). When we stay mindful of and surrendered to the Holy Spirit, peace will be the result. We don't have to strive for it. We don't have to make finding fruit of the Spirit another item on our to-do list. We just get to walk in step with Him. That is, we get to let God's Word and Spirit guide us moment by moment, day by day, one step at a time.

Look up Isaiah 26:12 and 1 Thessalonians 5:23. When it comes to experiencing peace, how do these verses help you focus on God's power and not your own effort?

SCRIPTURE MEMORY MOMENT

Write out 2 Thessalonians 3:16 and think about how God has already displayed the fruit of peace in your life.

A PRAYER FOR TODAY

GOD, *thank You that I don't have to conjure up peace on my own. And thank You that I don't have to navigate this rocky life alone. Holy Spirit, I recognize Your presence and Your power. What a gift You are! I'm so grateful that You choose to take up residence in my heart and that You promise to help me and teach me. Oh, how I need all the counsel You offer. Please continue to mold my heart with Your peace, convict me of unconfessed or hidden sin, and help me to walk in cadence with You. Amen.*

DAY 4

I will remember the deeds of the LORD;
    yes, I will remember your miracles of long ago.
I will consider all your works
    and meditate on all your mighty deeds.

Psalm 77:11–12 NIV

How is remembering God's faithfulness connected to your sense of peace?

_____

_____

_____

_____

_____

A promise is meant to be remembered. Pretty basic, but wouldn't you agree? When two people make marriage vows, committing to love and cherish each other forever, that's a promise they expect to keep coming back to. If you're a parent, you've probably heard the words "But you promised!" screeched out in a woe-is-me whine from a disappointed child who didn't get what you said they would.

As people, we can be promise breakers. We can also be broken by the broken promises of others. But God never breaks a promise. He never goes back on His word or pulls a bait and switch to His own benefit. Nope. He is faithful without fault.

Remembering who God is, what He has done, and what He has promised to do is essential to cultivating a heart of peace.

In this week's opening story on day 1, Jen shared how important it was for her family to remember God's Word in their season of unemployment and financial hardship. Recalling how He had come through in the past and rehearsing those powerful words from John 14:27 buoyed Jen's peace in the present and hope for the future. "Peace I leave with you. My peace I give to you." Shouldn't we all make that a refrain on repeat as the soundtrack of our days?

Especially when our circumstances don't feel peaceful—when our child is bullied or our neighbor seems unreasonable, when racism rears its ugly head or sin wreaks havoc on church leadership—we have the opportunity to cling to God's promise to give us peace no matter what.

Do you remember what the angels said when they announced the Savior's birth? *Peace on earth.*

Guess what Zechariah (John the Baptist's father) prophesied just six months earlier?

> Because of our God's merciful compassion,
> the dawn from on high will visit us
> to shine on those who live in darkness
> and the shadow of death,
> to guide our feet into the way of *peace*. (Luke 1:78–79)

This is God's promise. Jesus came to bring light into our dark places. He came to guide us in the way of peace.

Luke 1:67–79 records Zechariah's first words after being mute during the miracle pregnancy of his wife Elizabeth. Think about what you would want to say if you were suddenly able to speak after nine months. What does Zechariah's example tell you about the importance of remembering and giving voice to what God has done?

Read Psalm 119:49–56. What stands out to you from this passage related to the impact of remembering?

The whole Bible is basically a road map to the way remembering is crucial to following God, growing in faith, and living in peace. God knows that we're painfully forgetful, so He keeps beating the drum of remembrance.

In Joshua 3, we find the story of when the Israelites finally crossed the Jordan River into the promised land. Did they cross in boats or on rafts? No. They walked through on dry ground—because as soon as the priests carrying the ark of the covenant stepped into the water, God stopped the river's flow until all the people crossed over. God, who had promised to make a way, made a way!

Imagine for a moment what it would have been like for the people making that impossible, miraculous journey. To look to your right and see a wall of water. To look to your left and see dry ground. To know that you were in the middle of a miracle. Surely that's an experience you would never forget.

Yet . . . God knows how quickly and easily spiritual amnesia can set in. So as soon as the entire nation of Israel had crossed the Jordan, God told Joshua to have twelve men gather twelve stones from the middle of the river and set them up as a memorial in the place where the priests had stood. *Before* they sat down to rest. *Before* they scouted the new territory or chose a place to set up camp, God wanted His people to mark the miracle. He told them to create a physical reminder of His faithfulness so that when things got rough or another impossible barrier arose, they would remember the one who guides them and brings them peace.

> **Read Joshua 4:1–10. Why do you think God commanded that stones be gathered from the middle of the Jordan rather than from on shore? Why do you think constructing this memorial was an urgent task?**

Fast-forward more than fourteen hundred years to the night of the Last Supper, and we find the most poignant call to remember. On that night Jesus would be betrayed and arrested, but first He ate the Passover meal with His closest friends.

> And he took bread, gave thanks, broke it, gave it to them, and said, "This is my body, which is given for you. Do this in

> remembrance of me." In the same way he also took the cup after supper and said, "This cup is the new covenant in my blood, which is poured out for you." (Luke 22:19–20)

Do this in remembrance of me.

Jesus gave us a ritual for retention. A way to not forget. A way to tangibly train our hearts and minds to rehearse His goodness. To point ourselves back to the center, to the one who is before all things and who holds all things together (Col. 1:17).

The practice of eating a bit of bread or cracker and drinking a sip of wine or juice is a practice in hearing the voice of our Savior.

> *Don't forget I loved you so much that I allowed My body to be broken for you.*
> *Don't forget I loved you so much that I allowed My blood to be poured out for you.*
> *Don't forget I overcame death and conquered the world so you could have peace on earth and peace with Me forever.*

Intentionally remembering is the path to a heart of peace.

How do you feel when you read the italicized words above that express Jesus's heart for you? Read Psalm 77:11–12. How would meditating on what Christ did on the cross affect your peace?

_____

_____

_____

_____

SCRIPTURE MEMORY MOMENT

Write out 2 Thessalonians 3:16 and remember how God's peace has been with you. If you have time, write the verse three more times in your journal.

A PRAYER FOR TODAY

LORD JESUS, *I remember. I remember Your love and Your sacrifice. I remember how You made a way for the Israelites to cross the Jordan and how You've made a way for me in impossible situations. Thank You that the promises in Your Word are trustworthy. When peace feels far away and fear threatens to cloud my vision, help me to remember who You are and what You've done. I love You. Amen.*

DAY 5

Trust in him at all times, you people;
  pour out your hearts to him,
  for God is our refuge.

Psalm 62:8 NIV

What keeps you from trusting God? Are there times you feel like you can't share your whole self or your current struggle with Him?

Can I share with you a passage that makes my heart feel most at peace? It doesn't describe a serene setting or a life free of struggle. The word *peace* isn't even used. The most peace-giving words to me are an invitation from Jesus:

> Come to me, all you who are weary and burdened, and I will give you rest. Take my yoke upon you and learn from me, for I am gentle and humble in heart, and you will find rest for your souls. For my yoke is easy and my burden is light. (Matt. 11:28–30 NIV)

Do you feel your soul exhale as you read those words?

Jesus doesn't say don't be weary. He doesn't tell us to fix or hide or overcome our burdens. He just invites us to come. He understands that we will be worn-out and weighed down by life. He expects it! Does this go against the picture of cleaned-up Christianity you've been asked to emulate? If so, it's time to get a different picture.

A surefire way *not* to experience the peace of Jesus is to live like it's all up to you. If you keep trying to carry your burdens all by yourself, if you keep trying to medicate your weariness with more caffeine, more shopping, more alcohol, or harder hustling, you'll undoubtedly end up with sore shoulders and an aching soul.

We weren't meant to do it all alone.

Whatever you're carrying today, Jesus wants to carry it with you. He wants to shoulder the weight of your broken heart. He wants to bear the burden of the abuse or prejudice you've experienced. He wants to hold your unanswered questions and strained family relationships. He wants to walk with you through your illness or rocky marriage or over-whelming responsibilities at work.

> **Read Matthew 11:28–30 from The Message (you can find this easily using a Bible app or at Biblegateway.com). What words stand out to you? Take a moment to quiet your soul. What is Jesus saying to you?**

Do you feel like you have to carry your burdens alone? What keeps you from releasing your fears or weariness to Jesus?

_____

_____

_____

_____

The result of Christ's peace is rest for our souls. Taking Christ's yoke upon us is a picture of hitching ourselves to Jesus, like two oxen who share one wooden crosspiece that joins them together. It means learning to follow Christ's cadence, learning to make our steps match His.

He promises that being joined to Him is easier than forging ahead on our own. He promises to give us rest for our souls. Doesn't that sound like peace?

Jesus's promise reverberates as it echoes the words of His forefather King David:

> Truly my soul finds rest in God;
>   my salvation comes from him. (Ps. 62:1 NIV)

Soul rest differs from physical rest. You can get a full eight hours of sleep and still wake up without peace. You can spend the day at the beach or getting lost in a novel and still have an anxious soul. Soul rest

Soul rest is marked by a deep assurance and trust that God is present and working on your behalf.

is marked by a deep assurance and trust that God is present and working on your behalf.

> **Read all of Psalm 62. What evidence do you see of God being present and trustworthy? What does David encourage people to do in verse 8?**

_____

_____

_____

_____

Do you want God to create in you a heart of peace? Me too, sister. That's why we have to trust in Him. Not sometimes. Not occasionally. At _all_ times. And we have to—we _get_ to—pour out our hearts to Him. We get to tell Him all the junk that's tangling us up. We get to share every detail of that thing we're wrestling with. We get to uncover our shame and fear and mistakes. We get to whisper every dream and desire and secret need.

When we do, we can then rest in the peace and comfort of God's refuge.

He's a safe place to land, a sanctuary of protection.

We are secure in Him.

You, friend, are secure in Him.

Let His peace wash over you like a river. Let it lap up on the shore of your heart. Let it lighten your load and guide you in taking the next step.

Jesus is humble and gentle. Let Him lead the way.

What most resonated with you from this day (or week) of the study? What truth do you want to remember to cling to?

SCRIPTURE MEMORY MOMENT

Test yourself on 2 Thessalonians 3:16. Try to say it out loud and write it from memory. As we move into the next week of our study, hide these words in your heart and reflect on them often. Perhaps write 2 Thessalonians 3:16 on a sticky note and put it somewhere you'll see it every day.

A PRAYER FOR TODAY

JESUS, *I accept Your invitation to come. Thank You for loving me in my weariness. Thanks for accepting me in the middle of my mess and when I'm bogged down by burdens. Teach me, Jesus, to walk in step with You. Teach me to trust You more fully and to experience the soul rest You promise. I'm ready for a heart of lasting peace. Amen.*

PEACE IS A PRACTICE

Peace isn't a one-and-done kind of thing. It's not something to be conquered or a five-step course you can master. We've already discovered how peace is found first and foremost in the *person* of Jesus. It's also a *posture* we can hold and a *promise* we can cling to. And this week we'll unpack how peace is a *practice*. It's a moment-by-moment decision.

We experience the peace of God by praying, giving thanks, rejoicing in Him, and being purposeful in our thinking. Giving God full access to our hearts and allowing His peace to flourish in us require that we live with expectancy and make practicing peace part of our daily rhythm.

In today's story, we see how important it is to have a foundation of peace practices, especially when a crisis hits. (in)courage writer Robin Dance shares about an unexpected season when she needed God's peace more than ever before. Pay close attention to what Robin shares at the end about the key to experiencing a kind of peace that didn't match her circumstances.

A Story of Peace

It was Valentine's Day, but I was feeling a little blue. I was still grieving the loss of our family's long tradition of a mother-daughter Valentine tea. What began as a thoughtful suggestion by my precious mother-in-law when my daughter Rachel was three had continued each year into Rachel's twenties. Our tea—never limited to just tea—was a celebration of love among three generations of women. Almost as soon as one year's celebration ended, we were already cheerfully anticipating the next year's gathering of family and friends.

But eventually our annual Valentine tea slipped quietly into history with little fanfare. Slowly—and yet seemingly overnight—my mother-in-law's mind had become trapped in dementia's snare.

Given our mother-daughter tradition, I had long before stopped viewing Valentine's Day as a strictly romantic observance. Consequently, my husband was off the hook for lavishing me with flowers or chocolate. Still, ever a words-of-encouragement girl, I always treasured his cards.

Now, with my former tradition sidelined, my focus shifted back toward him. How might we celebrate?

Neither of us was interested in going out to a crowded restaurant, so we planned a simple steak dinner at home. Spinach salad with berries and balsamic dressing, baked potatoes with all the fixings, a filet for me and a ribeye for him. Tad can grill a steak like nobody's business, and I was already smacking my lips in anticipation.

Until I remembered our grill was broken. The part we needed for the repair hadn't yet arrived.

Undeterred, I changed up our menu. I'd stir-fry a sirloin the way my father had when I was little, with lots of black pepper and a pile of sliced onions. It wasn't Tad's favorite, but it was still steak, and for me it held a sweet association with my childhood.

The first hint something was wrong came shortly after dinner. My husband complained about indigestion, an issue he seldom experiences. He just as quickly brushed it off, attributing whatever was going on to taking over-the-counter cold meds earlier in the day.

We resumed our movie watching (I'm the fortunate wife who's married to a guy who likes a good Meg Ryan / Tom Hanks rom-com), but a while later I noticed him holding his upper arm.

"Does your left arm hurt?!" I blurted.

"A little, but it comes and goes," he admitted, minimizing his own worries but having little effect on mine.

"YOU'RE HAVING A HEART ATTACK!" I shrieked, flinging open my laptop to search "cardiac arrest symptoms." He insisted he was fine and scoffed at Dr. Google's credentials. I countered that he was *not* fine and we needed to go to the ER. My pleas to seek medical attention were about as effective as his attempts to dismiss my concerns.

It was understandable that he wasn't taking this seriously. Under fifty and in good health, he had no family history of heart disease. *Was I unreasonable for jumping to conclusions?*

After the movie, I crawled into bed, still unsettled and whispering a looping prayer. *Please keep Tad safe, give us Your wisdom, prompt us to act if needed.* Somehow, I drifted to sleep.

You might say I won the argument when at 3:30 a.m. we were on our way to the emergency room. Barely an hour later, our suspicions were confirmed. The cardiologist on call swished back the privacy curtain, mounted a stool, swiveled to face us, drew a deep breath, and delivered the news. Though he couldn't be sure exactly what had happened until further testing, the lab results pointed to a "cardiac event," a nice way of telling us my husband had experienced a heart attack.

It felt like we were watching a movie. Or somebody else's life. This wasn't the kind of thing that happened to us.

That is, until it did.

I felt like we were in the eye of a hurricane. An inexplicable calm surrounded my husband and me, and I wondered when the backside of the storm would whip around and lash us to pieces.

As the medical staff tended to Tad, my natural reflex was to pray. This was no atheist-in-a-foxhole moment. I knew how badly I—*we*—needed God's presence to face the next few hours. And I *knew* beyond shadows and doubts that He was with us because the peace He promises in Philippians 4:6–7 was exactly what we were experiencing: "Don't worry about anything, but in everything, through prayer and petition with thanksgiving, present your requests to God. And the peace of God, which surpasses all understanding, will guard your hearts and minds in Christ Jesus."

Peace that surpasses all understanding.

At the first chance I got, I enlisted a legion of prayer warriors, inviting family and friends to battle with us. What they offered through God's Word, their own words of encouragement, and prayer were weapons of heavenly proportion.

It astounded me, really, how calm both Tad and I remained as we learned more about what had already happened and was yet to take place. Paul's words in Philippians 4:9 contain the key: "Do what you have learned and received and heard from me, and seen in me, and the God of peace will be with you."

For most of our lives, Tad and I have attended church; we've studied the Bible in group settings and on our own. We've learned, received, and heard from Jesus through Scripture and in sound teaching.

So when a life-threatening scenario played out in front of us, we didn't resort to prayer out of panic or fear; we responded in faithfulness with an already established practice. Praying united us with God and ushered His presence into the midst of our circumstances, and then His peace—a peace that doesn't begin to make sense—guarded our hearts and minds.

God always delivers what He promises. The natural rhythm of prayer in our lives makes way for His supernatural peace.

Not just on Valentine's Day but 365 days a year.

—ROBIN DANCE

Can you think of a time when your peace didn't reflect your circumstances? How did God's peace guard your heart and mind?

Read Psalm 18:1–6. How does the psalmist David approach God? What
does David do and how does God respond?

Is there an area of your life in distress? Do you feel free to pour out your
heart to God? Why or why not? How might coming to God in both heartfelt praise and unfiltered honesty lead you to peace?

SCRIPTURE MEMORY MOMENT

This week's memory verses are Philippians 4:6–7. Write out the verses in your journal (as printed here from the NLT or from your favorite translation). Throughout the week, commit these words to memory as you ask God to create in you a heart of peace through the daily rhythm of prayer.

Don't worry about anything; instead, pray about everything. Tell God what you need, and thank him for all he has done. Then you will experience God's peace, which exceeds anything we can understand. His peace will guard your hearts and minds as you live in Christ Jesus.

A PRAYER FOR TODAY

GOD, *thank You for always being with me in the regular challenges of everyday life and in times of crisis. I believe that Your peace is available to me. Train my heart to practice turning to You in prayer and thanksgiving so I may experience Your peace that surpasses understanding. Oh, Jesus, I know my peace is in You. Keep molding my heart this week and marking it with Your peace. Amen.*

Pray in the Spirit at all times and on every occasion. Stay alert and be persistent in your prayers for all believers everywhere.

Ephesians 6:18 NLT

Is it easier for you to pray when life is going well or in times of crisis? Why do you think that is?

Prayer is a cornerstone of the Christian life. It's our main mode of communication with God. If we're going to be in relationship with someone, we have to talk to them—and listen. It sounds so basic, and it is. But in the same way roommates or spouses can become like passing ships, occupying the same waters but never pausing to really engage and see the other, we too can forget to communicate with God.

We can be like a teenager who doesn't call their parent until they're out of gas and stranded on the side of the road. As a loving Father, God will take our panicked call. He'll hear our cry. But if we want to live a life of peace, we won't wait till we're desperate to talk to Him.

The story of Daniel illustrates the power of making prayer a regular rhythm. You're probably familiar with the epic tale of the man who survived the lions' den. But do you know what led up to it?

Let's read Daniel 6:1–18 to understand the backstory.

Daniel was in an impossible situation based on the king's order. What did Daniel do as soon as he learned the document had been signed? What do you learn about the rhythm of Daniel's life from verse 10?

When have you been in an impossible situation? What was your first feeling or response?

We can only imagine how distraught Daniel must have felt upon hearing that he would be thrown to the lions if he continued to worship and pray to the one true God. As Christians living in the Western world, we may never have to choose between loyalty to God and life. But that's exactly the decision Daniel faced. And in this watershed moment, Daniel turned to God the same way he always had: "Three times a day he got down on his knees, prayed, and gave thanks to his God, just as he had done before" (Dan. 6:10).

Just as he had done before.

The text doesn't specifically say Daniel was at peace. But in this beautiful picture of submission and gratitude, we see Daniel *practicing* peace. Three times a day he entered into a conversation with God. He shared his heart, his fears, his predicament. He affirmed his trust, his surrender, his obedience. Daniel praised God for who He is and thanked Him for what He had already done *and* for what He would yet do.

Indeed, Daniel modeled the exact instructions the apostle Paul would pen centuries later. It's our Scripture memory passage for the week: "Don't worry about anything, but in everything, through prayer and petition with thanksgiving, present your requests to God. And the peace of God, which surpasses all understanding, will guard your hearts and minds in Christ Jesus" (Phil. 4:6–7).

Since we know God is true to His Word, we can have confidence in concluding that the peace of God surrounded Daniel the day he found out King Darius made a law against praying to anyone besides the king.

When we continue reading the story in Daniel 6:19–28, we learn that Daniel was indeed thrown into the pit of lions and that God sent an angel to close the beasts' jaws. Daniel escaped unscathed. And the king overturned his edict and instead issued a new decree that all people must serve Daniel's living God. Yes, this is miraculous! But my favorite part of Daniel's story? Seeing the peace of God reign in the middle of the impossible—which began when Daniel prayed.

> Read Matthew 14:23, Mark 1:35, and Luke 5:16. What do these verses say that Jesus did? What role do you think prayer played in Jesus's life, ministry, and peace?

From the New Testament accounts of Jesus's life as recorded in the Gospels, it's clear that prayer was a regular practice for God's Son. Jesus prayed for many reasons, but a primary purpose, just like everything Jesus did in His thirty-three earthbound years, was to serve as a model for what it looks like to cultivate continual, intimate connection with the Father. Though Jesus was Himself fully God, He showed us what it looks like to live dependent on and surrendered to the Father's will and the Holy Spirit's power. When Jesus was tempted in the wilderness, He prayed. When Jesus was in the thick of a grueling ministry schedule, He prayed. When Jesus was suffering on the cross, He prayed. On ordinary days and in the throes of agony, Jesus demonstrated what it looks like to make prayer an intentional, consistent practice.

Jesus promised to give us peace. We receive it by patterning our lives after His.

When Robin found herself in the emergency room listening to the news that her husband had suffered a heart attack, prayer was her first response. Not because Robin was in a rare "help me, God" moment and willing to try anything in her desperation. Prayer naturally poured from Robin's heart because that was already her practice.

And the supernatural peace of God followed.

Read Psalm 5:3, Psalm 6:9, and Ephesians 6:18. How can you cultivate a practice of prayer this week? What peace does it give you to know God hears your prayers?

SCRIPTURE MEMORY MOMENT

Write out Philippians 4:6–7. How will you fix your thoughts on God this week? Now text this passage to a friend who might be encouraged by it. Invite her to memorize it with you!

A PRAYER FOR TODAY

GOD, *thank You for hearing my cries for help—on a regular Tuesday and in times of crisis. What a profound gift that You invite me to share my heart with You and listen to Your voice in response. Grow me in the practice of prayer this week. Not as another task to check off a spiritual to-do list but as a way to deepen my relationship with You and experience Your peace. Amen.*

DAY 3

Rejoice always, pray constantly, give thanks in everything; for
this is God's will for you in Christ Jesus.

1 Thessalonians 5:16–18

**What are you thankful for today? Try to reach past the obvious and write
down five situations or circumstances in which you're choosing gratitude, including some that aren't so easy.**

_____

_____

_____

_____

_____

We're more than halfway through our study, and today we're going to
connect the dots back to some of the foundational truths we've already
covered.

On day 4 of week 3, we looked at Zechariah's prophetic words about
Jesus: "Because of God's tender mercy, the morning light from heaven
is about to break upon us, to give light to those who sit in darkness and
in the shadow of death, and to guide us to the path of peace" (Luke

1:78–79 NLT). The contrast between light and dark refers foremost to the salvation of our souls; in God's mercy, He sent Jesus to allow people to cross from death to life. In this, Jesus becomes the way to eternal peace. But remember what the angels declared the night Christ was born? *"Peace on earth."* The way of Jesus leads not only to peace everlasting but also to peace in the everyday.

So what does peace in the everyday look like? When bills are piling up and prejudice is searing, when a child has another ear infection or a friend gets in a devastating accident, how do we stay on the path of peace?

Paul tells us in the closing of his first letter to the church at Thessalonica, "Rejoice always, pray constantly, give thanks in everything; for this is God's will for you in Christ Jesus" (1 Thess. 5:16–18).

"For this is God's will for you in Christ Jesus." Those words should be like flashing neon lights telling us to pay attention. Paul's instructions are clear: *Rejoice always. Pray constantly. Give thanks in everything.*

Paul doesn't say do these things and your life will be easy. Or do these things and God will give you everything you want. He says do these things and you'll know you are following the will of God.

Of the three components of Paul's instructions in 1 Thessalonians 5:16–18, which one comes most naturally for you? Which one is the hardest? Why do you think that's the case?

Why do you think God wants us to be joyful always, pray continually, and be thankful in all circumstances? Think about the most peaceful person you know. Do they practice these instructions?

_____

_____

_____

_____

Paul then goes on to say, "Now may the God of peace himself sanctify you completely. And may your whole spirit, soul, and body be kept sound and blameless at the coming of our Lord Jesus Christ. He who calls you is faithful; he will do it" (1 Thess. 5:23–24).

In other words, as you choose to live in God's will, He will be faithful to work in you! _The God of peace Himself_ will intervene in your life and mold your heart to sanctify you—that is, make you holy and set apart. Sister, this means you can rest in Jesus!

God wants to teach us how to pattern our lives after Jesus so we can experience the fullness of His love, mercy, and peace. But ultimately God is the one who does the work in us.

Pressure off. Peace on.

Paul understood how significant this truth is, so he wove it into his other letters to build up believers in other churches. To the church in Philippi, he wrote:

> I give thanks to my God for every remembrance of you, always praying with joy for all of you in my every prayer, because of your partnership in the gospel from the first day until now. I am sure of this, that he who started a good work in you will carry it on to completion until the day of Christ Jesus. (Phil. 1:3–6)

Philippians was written about five years after 1 Thessalonians, and do you see what Paul is practicing? He's practicing exactly what he preached.

Look at the above passage from Philippians 1. Circle or underline the phrases that correspond with Paul's instructions in 1 Thessalonians (rejoice, pray, give thanks). What stands out to you from Paul's encouragement in Philippians?

As I've been implementing Paul's teaching in my own life, I've discovered a connecting thread between rejoicing, praying, and giving thanks: each one of these practices invites (forces) me to shift my focus from myself to God. For example, rejoicing leads me to consider God's character—what is He like, and why can I trust Him? Praying reminds me that I'm not alone. Giving thanks requires that I stop grumbling to myself and instead express gratitude to God, who is good—always.

Do you see what I mean? We cannot do these things apart from Him! And, friends, we were never meant to.

Our memory verse this week is Philippians 4:6–7, which reminds us again how integral prayer and thanksgiving are to receiving God's peace. But back up just two verses and we find this call to action: "Rejoice in the Lord always. I will say it again: Rejoice!" (v. 4).

When I think about the times in my life when peace felt fleeting or out of reach, rejoicing wasn't easy. This must be why Paul keeps reminding us to do it! He knows our default response is to fixate on our circumstances, turn inward to our own feelings, or focus on our own ability to fix the problem.

But Jesus calls us to a different way. Through His Word, He's telling us:

> *Rejoice! Remember who I am. Let My joy fill you up.*
> *Pray! Talk to Me. I'm here listening. You can trust Me with all of your burdens and cares.*
> *Give thanks! Turn your pleas to praise as you acknowledge all that I've done and will yet do.*

Read those words again, friend. Let them wash over you like an invitation, not another obligation. A grace-filled arrow pointing you to peace.

Read Philippians 4:9. What have you learned this week that you want to put into practice?

SCRIPTURE MEMORY MOMENT

Write out Philippians 4:6–7 and think about what it means to pray and give thanks *in everything*. How does rejoicing prepare your heart to do this?

A PRAYER FOR TODAY

JESUS! *Oh, how I love You. Thank You for being my peace forever and my peace for today. Help me to put into practice the guidelines for peaceful living You've laid out in Your Word. When I'm tempted to withhold my joy or thanks, help me to shift my focus from my circumstances to Your goodness. Transform my heart from anxious and fearful to trusting and peaceful—one praise, one prayer, one grateful word at a time. Amen.*

DAY 4

Set your minds on things above, not on earthly things.

Colossians 3:2

What occupies most of your thought life? List the top five things you most often find yourself contemplating or ruminating on.

_____

_____

_____

_____

_____

God made our minds and emotions beautiful, dynamic, and complex. He knows that what dominates our thoughts will have direct implications for our ability to communicate with Him in prayer and to experience joy, gratitude, and ultimately _peace_.

In His love, God wants to protect our minds and hearts. But we have to partner with Him. We do this by living out this week's key verses from Philippians 4:6–7: "Don't worry about anything, but in everything, through prayer and petition with thanksgiving, present your requests to God." (We'll keep going over this because it's so crucial to the full and peaceful life God promises!) When we intentionally move our minds from worry to surrender, from self-focus to God-focus, then the miraculous happens: "And the peace of God, which surpasses all understanding, will guard your hearts and minds in Christ Jesus."

Yesterday we talked about the importance of rejoicing, praying, and giving thanks. Today we'll take it a step further and learn how these three things hinge on the simple and powerful practice of thinking.

Thinking? How is that a practice? Valid question. Let's listen to Paul for the answer:

> Finally brothers and sisters, whatever is true, whatever is honorable, whatever is just, whatever is pure, whatever is lovely, whatever is commendable—if there is any moral excellence and if there is anything praiseworthy—dwell on these things. Do what you have learned and received and heard from me, and seen in me, and the God of peace will be with you. (Phil. 4:8–9)

Our peace is tied to how we discipline our minds. Dwell on fear, worry, gossip, and unmet desires, and surely peace will elude you. Fix your mind on the dark scroll of social media comparison and disparaging news stories, and surely the state of your heart and mind will mirror those things. In the same way, if you think about truth, beauty, justice, and holiness, your mind will reflect the peace of God!

In the New Living Translation, Philippians 4:8 is translated, "Think about things that are excellent and worthy of praise." What (or who) is worthy of your praise today? How would thinking about that affect your peace?

Do you think these instructions to dwell on what's good means to stuff down or gloss over the hard things in life? Read Psalm 34. What examples do you see of crying out to God in honesty while also thinking about His goodness?

_____

_____

_____

_____

Make no mistake, dwelling on what is pure and lovely doesn't mean discounting the very real and ugly realities we often face in this world. God isn't asking us to ignore racism or abuse. He's not directing us to stop thinking about the hungry and homeless and vulnerable among us. He's not saying to stop grieving a loss or working toward restoration. If all you can think about today is pain or sorrow, God understands. He is right there with you.

But in Philippians 4:8, Paul is instructing us regarding what we allow to consume our thoughts on a regular basis. On an ordinary Thursday while you commute to work or change a load of laundry, while you pump gas or play Candyland with your toddler, what are you thinking about? As you quiet your soul in the steamy shower or fall asleep at night, what pictures or ideas fill your mind? In the everyday moments of our lives, we have the opportunity to practice peace by thinking about the things of God.

In the everyday moments of our lives, we have the opportunity to practice peace by thinking about the things of God.

I love that the first adjective Paul uses in his list of things we ought to think about is *true* (Phil. 4:9). A lot of untruth, partial truth, and subjective truth is circulating in our world today. It can be hard to know what stories and news sources are reliable. What information is trustworthy? Who can we be sure is telling the truth?

In a time when what is *un*lovely and *dis*honorable can bombard us, here are five true things to dwell on today:

1. **God loves you.** (John 3:16; Rom. 8:38–39; 1 John 4:9–10)
2. **God is working on your behalf.** (Rom. 8:28; Phil. 1:6; 2:13)
3. **Your future is secure in Him.** (Ps. 103:1–5; Prov. 3:5–6; Jer. 29:11–13)
4. **God will always be with you.** (Deut. 31:6, 8; Josh. 1:9; Isa. 41:10)
5. **God is faithful.** (Exod. 34:6; Lam. 3:22–23; 1 Thess. 5:23–24)

Which of those five truths do you most need to cling to today? Look up the three passages next to that promise and write down the one that resonates with you most.

_____

_____

_____

_____

Practicing peace requires intentionality. Just like you have to make an effort to take care of your physical body, you also have to be deliberate about caring for your spiritual well-being. We all know how easy it is to get to the end of the day and realize you didn't drink enough water— even though you know it's good for you. To stay hydrated, you have to keep drinking throughout the day. Make a plan. Follow through. The same is true for staying on track with your thought life. It's not a one-and-done kind of decision. It's a moment-by-moment, continual commitment to training your focus on Jesus.

In Colossians 3:2, Paul instructs us, "Set your minds on things above, not on earthly things." It's an invitation to an eternal perspective. Don't just think about what's happening right in front of you—the phone call you need to make, the errand you need to run, the misunderstanding you need to sort out. Think about what is true forever!

Elsewhere Paul explains it this way: "For our momentary light affliction is producing for us an absolutely incomparable eternal weight of glory. So we do not focus on what is seen, but on what is unseen. For what is seen is temporary, but what is unseen is eternal" (2 Cor. 4:17–18).

Friend, I'll be honest. Focusing on what is unseen isn't easy. What I can see today is my son struggling with anger. I can see my hip that needs surgery and my friend who is moving away. I can see the pain of injustice and the fear of another mass shooting. I can see a leak in our ceiling and a crack in our windshield.

God cares about what concerns me, and He cares about what concerns you. But through His Word, He's also lifting our chins and asking us to see *Him*. To see that the things we are dealing with today won't always be this way but that He will always be present and faithful and make His peace available to us.

We just need to turn our gaze and fix it on Him.

> Return to our list of five true things we can dwell on today. Choose another one of those truths and look up the designated verses. How could fixing your mind on these promises change your perspective and peace?

SCRIPTURE MEMORY MOMENT

Write out Philippians 4:6–7 and consider how God has been faithful to guard your heart and mind with His peace. If you have time, write the verses three more times in your journal.

A PRAYER FOR TODAY

GOD, *thank You for loving me in the middle of my hard and ordinary days. Thank You for loving me in my imperfections and for being faithful to walk with me. Please help me to train my mind to focus on what is true and pure and commendable. Help me to remember that any trial I face today is temporary and my future is secure in You. Keep creating in me a heart of peace! I commit to partnering with You. Amen.*

DAY 5

Those who love your instructions have great peace
and do not stumble.

Psalm 119:165 NLT

How has your time in God's Word through this study affected your peace? What do you notice about how you think and feel after meditating on Scripture?

_____

_____

_____

_____

_____

If we could devote ourselves to only a single practice, it ought to be the practice of spending time in God's Word. This may seem obvious, given that you've chosen to do this Bible study. But it's worth shining a spotlight on what God's Word has to say about itself and the effect it is designed to have on our peace.

We've already spent quite a bit of time in the book of Psalms, but it's a great place for us to land again today because these songs and poems show us what a growing relationship with God looks like in the midst of real and often difficult circumstances. The Psalms remind us that God hears our cries and is present in our distress. The Psalms also display a repetitive theme of God's Word as our life source.

Psalm 1 begins:

> Oh, the joys of those who do not
>   follow the advice of the wicked,
>   or stand around with sinners,
>   or join in with mockers.
> But they delight in the law of the LORD,
>   meditating on it day and night.
> They are like trees planted along the riverbank,
>   bearing fruit each season.
> Their leaves never wither,
>   and they prosper in all they do. (vv. 1–3 NLT)

Other translations say, "How happy is the one" (CSB) or "Blessed is the one" (NIV) who delights in God's law. I love the imagery of being like a tree planted right next to a water source. Picture thirsty roots growing deep into the soil, soaking up every bit of life-giving water and nutrients. The tree's branches stretch high to the sun. You know this tree is healthy because it bears fruit in season—delicious evidence that it's alive and being exactly what it was created to be!

This is a picture of how we are meant to thrive as women rooted in Scripture. When we nourish ourselves in God's Word—not out of religious duty or obligation but out of *delight*—we will prosper and overflow with joy. That joy plus deep faith that God is still working on our behalf—even when life gets hard—*that* sounds like peace to me.

Read Psalm 19:7–9. Record the attributes of Scripture and their impact on our lives.

	Attribute	Impact
v. 7		
v. 8		
v. 9		

What keeps you motivated to consistently read your Bible? What barriers prevent or discourage you from spending time in God's Word?

God wants us to fall in love with the gift of His Word!

The opening of Psalm 119 echoes Psalm 1: "How happy are those whose way is blameless, who walk according to the LORD's instruction! Happy are those who keep his decrees and seek him with all their heart" (vv. 1–2). There's a direct correlation between reading, studying, and following God's instructions and our emotional, mental, and spiritual well-being.

With 176 verses, Psalm 119 is the longest chapter in the entire Bible. And can you guess what every verse is about? Delighting in God's Word. When you have time, it's absolutely worth going slowly through each verse. For today, consider the beauty of verse 165: "Those who love your instructions have great peace and do not stumble" (NLT).

It doesn't say those who spend forty-five minutes reading a devotional and praying first thing every morning have peace. It doesn't say those who never mess up or who never have hard days have peace. It says those who love God's instructions have *great* peace. God wants us to fall in love with the gift of His Word!

If I were to write down everything I wanted my children to know—every instruction for wise living, every reminder of how fiercely I love them—and if that was the primary way they would hear from me, I would want them to read every word. I'd hope they would love listening to my voice and would heed my counsel. Can you imagine how much more God our Father feels about the written record of love and guidance He has given us?

Read Psalm 119:105–112. Where do you need God's Word to light your path today? Turn these verses into a personal prayer.

In his second letter to Timothy, a beloved friend, ministry partner, and spiritual son, Paul offers this powerful reminder: "All Scripture is inspired by God and is useful to teach us what is true and to make us realize what is wrong in our lives. It corrects us when we are wrong and teaches us to do what is right. God uses it to prepare and equip his people to do every good work" (2 Tim. 3:16–17 NLT).

Paul and Timothy had traveled together for years over countless miles. They had enjoyed seasons of abundant ministry and endured harsh trials and persecution. Paul loved Timothy like a son; he wanted to impart every bit of wisdom he had. And Paul knew that the very best thing he could do was to direct Timothy back to Scripture. More than any advice he could give, Paul knew that Timothy—like each one of us— needed to be instructed by God's very Word.

To become people of peace, we must be people who delight in hearing from God. The best way we can do that is to commit ourselves to spending time reading the love letter and instructions for daily living He's so graciously given us in the Bible. God-breathed. God-inspired. Useful for every aspect of our lives. It's a practice that will surely lead us to His peace.

> **"May God give you more and more grace and peace as you grow in your knowledge of God and Jesus our Lord" (2 Pet. 1:2 NLT). How do you want to grow in your knowledge of God? What practice will you begin (or continue) so that learning through Scripture is a priority in your life?**

SCRIPTURE MEMORY MOMENT

Test yourself on Philippians 4:6–7. Try to say it out loud and write it from memory. As we move into the next week of our study, hide these words in your heart and reflect on them often. Perhaps write Philippians 4:6–7 on a sticky note and put it somewhere you'll see it every day.

A PRAYER FOR TODAY

LORD, *thank You for the gift of Your Word! I delight in who You are and the instructions You have given. I want to be like the fruitful tree planted by a flowing stream. Grow my desire for Your Word. When I'm tempted to turn to a worldly source of peace, remind me instead to find solace and guidance in Your Word. What a good Father You are! Amen.*

PEACE IS AN OUTPOURING

Even when we *know* Jesus is the source of our peace, even when we practice gratitude and pray faithfully, anxiety and grief can still grip us. So is it wrong to worry? Does struggling through life indicate an insincere faith? What we'll discover in Scripture this week is that God welcomes our honesty, He accepts us in our weakness, and He affirms that we cannot receive lasting peace apart from Him.

In this week's story, (in)courage writer Bonnie Gray shares how the wounds of her past created a tendency to nurture others above herself and to try to control her circumstances. As you read, pay attention to the way God's comfort reaches Bonnie in the middle of her anxiety. If you've ever felt tempted to believe you have to get it together in order to experience God's peace, let this story minister to your soul. No matter where you are or what you're going through today, God is ready and willing to pour out His peace on you.

A Story of Peace

Anxiety grips me when I least expect it. A lump rises in my throat that I can't swallow down. My heart skips a beat, giving an odd flutter that feels like the wings of a butterfly caught in a glass jar. Even though I take a deep breath and pray continuously for God to restore calm, my body just doesn't feel well.

These moments are hard because, as a mom, I don't want my feelings of unrest to affect my kids. I smile, ask them how their homework is coming along. I open the fridge, take out food, and prepare dinner. I hide my heart. My husband is also working hard to take care of our family, and I don't want to be a burden to him. So I give him a hug and ask, "How's it going?"

I push through the day and tell myself this anxious feeling will pass. But deep inside I'm not okay. I devote myself to nurturing peace for my children, husband, and friends, yet inner peace eludes me.

This longing for peace hits me hardest at night, when everyone is tucked in bed and I know I should be asleep too. But I feel lonely and can't rest.

In my heart I cry out, *God, why is this happening? Why aren't You helping me?*

If I'm honest, the peace I want is the absence of my shortcomings. But God's peace is deeper. God's peace is loving me right in the moments when life is flawed—when *I* feel flawed.

It's hard to explain, but the kind of anxiety I experience isn't situational. I'm not anxious because I have a problem in my faith, my marriage, or my children. My anxiety surfaces when my body reminds me I need a deeper peace that doesn't come through solving problems or staying strong. It surfaces when I try to power through in survival mode by working hard and getting things done. As the oldest in my family growing up, I took on the role of being the responsible one, the one good at taking care of everyone else. My go-to coping mechanism became fixing whatever is wrong.

But I've learned on my journey of healing from emotional PTSD and childhood trauma that although God's grace enabled me to be strong and get through hard times earlier in my life, we weren't designed to carry our burdens indefinitely or ignore our emotional needs into adulthood.

Calming anxiety isn't about fixing problems. It's about receiving an outpouring of God's peace. What we really need from Him is something we can't get by being strong: comfort.

My therapist once asked me, "What is your first memory of being comforted?"

I was seven years old. My parents had just gotten divorced. My mother was working late restaurant hours and didn't get home until past midnight. I was taking care of my younger sister on my own, and then later at night we went to my grandma's to sleep until my mother picked us up.

I remember sleeping on a fold-up cot and being sick with a bad cough, the kind that hurts your chest and wakes you up right as you're falling asleep. I was crying because my head hurt every time I blew my nose, and as I looked out into the room, dark as molasses, I felt all alone.

As I cried into the pillow, I felt a gentle hand on my shoulder. Someone heard me coughing. Someone heard me crying. It was Grandma.

She brought some cool menthol salve. As she slowly guided me to sit up, I leaned onto my grandma and felt the soothing touch of her hand on my back, rubbing the sweet scent of menthol onto my skin and bringing me relief.

"It's okay." Grandma helped me lie back down. Wiped my tears. Tucked me in. "Grandma's here."

Grandma didn't say what I usually tell myself when I feel anxiety. Grandma didn't explain why I was coughing or say, "You'll be fine so stop crying." She didn't educate me on how long colds last or question why I was so worried.

Grandma comforted me.

Grandma's hands reassured me with her *touch*. Grandma *listened* to me. She *stayed* with me.

That night, my head still hurt. I didn't sleep much. But I no longer felt alone.

For that one moment, in my time of need, I felt loved.

Receiving God's peace requires us to be vulnerable. To tell the truth of how things really are, not how we wish them to be.

For me, learning to receive God's peace meant being more honest with myself than what I was comfortable with—my likes and dislikes, questions and doubts. It's only when I open the door to the things that I don't think anyone would love or find useful about me that I can receive the healing I need: being loved for just who I am, all parts of me.

Only then, in my place of honesty, can I hear Jesus tenderly whisper:

You don't have to be strong.

It's okay to feel anxious.

I understand you completely.

You are safe with Me.

Let Me be your peace.

—**BONNIE GRAY**

Answer the same question Bonnie answered in her story: What is your first memory of being comforted? Have you experienced this kind of comfort from the Lord?

What do the following verses say about who God is and what He does for us? How does thinking about His character lead you to peace?

Psalm 9:9–10

Psalm 46:1

Psalm 119:76

_____

_____

_____

_____

_____

What has your experience been with anxiety? Do you relate to feeling the need to fix and control every situation? In week 3, we read Matthew 11:28–30. Read that passage again along with Isaiah 41:10. How does God's invitation to come to Him in our weariness *and* His promise to strengthen us assure you that you actually aren't responsible for holding it all together—whatever your "it" may be?

_____

_____

_____

_____

SCRIPTURE MEMORY MOMENT

This week's memory verse is 2 Corinthians 1:3. Write out the verse in your journal (as printed here from the NLT or from your favorite translation). Throughout the week, commit these words to memory as you praise God for His strength and comfort, and ask Him to create in you a heart of peace.

All praise to God, the Father of our Lord Jesus Christ. God is our merciful Father and the source of all comfort.

A PRAYER FOR TODAY

JESUS, *thank You for whispering to my heart when I'm anxious or hurting or scared. Thank You for never leaving me alone or unequipped. Your comfort and strength are always available to me. Pour out Your peace in my life this week as I study Your Word. Amen.*

If I say, "My foot is slipping,"
your faithful love will support me, Lord.
When I am filled with cares,
your comfort brings me joy.

Psalm 94:18–19

When have you really felt God's comfort? Write down what was happening at the time and how you knew His faithful love was with you.

_____

_____

_____

_____

If there's a drum we should never get tired of beating, it's this: it's not about us.

Clap it out with me: It's. Not. About. Us.

If you have come to this study looking for practical ways to cultivate a more peaceful life, every one of those practices should point back to Christ. If you find yourself striving to ditch the worry and get your life under control so you can be calmer and have more peace, you might have missed the point. Peace isn't something you attain by striving. Peace is an outpouring of God's goodness.

Sharing a message he received from God about the coming Messiah, the prophet Isaiah writes:

> In all their suffering he also suffered,
>   and he personally rescued them.
> In his love and mercy he redeemed them.
>   He lifted them up and carried them
>   through all the years. (Isa. 63:9 NLT)

Whatever you're going through today, whatever pain you're enduring, grief you're bearing, or load you're carrying, Jesus understands your suffering. That's what makes His life, death, and resurrection so miraculous, so complete. Because Jesus experienced every bit of what it means to be human—birth from a mother, betrayal from a friend, thirst, hunger, love, anger, joy, temptation, and agonizing death—we can trust that He understands what we're going through. We can trust that His peace isn't trite or superficial. It's the peace of one who knows what it's like to be knotted up and knocked down. His peace lifts us up; it's Jesus who carries us.

Take a moment to take stock of your emotional, mental, and physical load. What weight are you carrying? Where do you feel like your feet are slipping?

Read Isaiah 40:1–11. How is God described? How are people described? What does this tell you about God's ability and desire to care for people?

_____

_____

_____

_____

I don't know about you, but when I'm in the throes of anxiety or dealing with a crisis or just bogged down by the slog of everyday life, I can start to believe things will always be this way. My current feelings will always overwhelm me, my current predicament will always be impossible to overcome. But Scripture tells us that we're like grass that withers and flowers that fade. Does this mean that our lives are inconsequential? No! This means that our troubles won't last forever—but God's Word and His goodness will remain.

Paul, a man well acquainted with hardship, described it like this: "For our light and momentary troubles are achieving for us an eternal glory that far outweighs them all" (2 Cor. 4:17 NIV). When Paul was being flogged or freezing in prison, I can't imagine those things felt either light or momentary. So was Paul downplaying his pain? Was he telling believers to slap on fake positivity? No. Paul was preaching from an eternal perspective. He was saying that no matter what you're dealing with today—a cough that's keeping you awake at night,

Our troubles won't last forever—but God's Word and His goodness will remain.

a family member who isn't emotionally available, a dream that's been shattered—God is with you, working through you, and preparing something that is so much better for you.

> Read 2 Corinthians 4:7–18. How does this passage describe the importance of Jesus's death and resurrection for how we handle daily hardships? How is it possible to outwardly waste away yet be inwardly renewed?

God is working on our behalf, and the hard things we're facing today will have lasting value. This doesn't mean that God *causes* our hardships. God isn't the source of cancer or layoffs, verbally abusive parents or broken marriages. But God is able to *redeem* our pain. If that's difficult for you to believe right now, I get it. Let's lean in to this additional truth and encouragement from Paul:

> Therefore, since we have been justified through faith, we have *peace with God through our Lord Jesus Christ*, through whom we have gained access by faith into this grace in which we now stand. And we boast in the hope of the glory of God. Not only so, but we also glory in our sufferings, because we know that suffering produces perseverance; perseverance, character; and character, hope. And hope does not put us to shame, because *God's love has been poured out into our hearts through the Holy Spirit*, who has been given to us. (Rom. 5:1–5 NIV)

There is purpose in what you're going through today. And it's possible that the very thing that feels like a barrier to your peace is actually what God is using to guide you to Him. Look at the italicized phrases in the above passage. God's peace through Jesus and God's love through the Holy Spirit are what encircle us in our suffering. Remember how it's not about us? God is the one who makes possible the journey from suffering to hope.

We began today's study with the words of Psalm 94:

> If I say, "My foot is slipping,"
> your faithful love will support me, LORD.
> When I am filled with cares,
> your comfort brings me joy. (vv. 18–19)

It's okay if you feel like your foot is slipping. It's okay if you've fallen down and cannot stand. Jesus, like the good shepherd He is, will gather you close to His heart and carry you. His peace is yours right where you are.

Read Romans 5:3–4. How have you seen the progression from suffering to hope play out in your life or in the life of someone you know? How does remembering the way God has worked in the past affect your peace today?

SCRIPTURE MEMORY MOMENT

Write out 2 Corinthians 1:3 and thank God for His mercy and comfort in your life. Now text the verse to a friend who might be encouraged by it. Invite her to memorize it with you!

A PRAYER FOR TODAY

GOOD FATHER, *my Shepherd Jesus, faithful Holy Spirit, thank You for being the ultimate source of my comfort and peace. I acknowledge that I don't have power to overcome today's challenges or secure tomorrow's future apart from You. I need You. Oh, how I need You. Thank You for promising to steady me when I slip and carry me when I can't go on. I love You. Amen.*

The Lνλλλ bless you
  and keep you;
the Lᴏʀᴅ make his face shine on you
  and be gracious to you;
the Lᴏʀᴅ turn his face toward you
  and give you peace.
                    Numbers 6:24–26 NIV

When have you felt the joy of someone who delighted in you? Maybe it was a parent, friend, or teacher. Describe that experience of knowing you were esteemed and supported just for being who you are.

Every night I sit on the edge of each of my sons' beds and pray for them. The words of Numbers 6:24–26 often make their way into my prayer. It's easy for me to claim this truth, this promise, over my children. As their mom, I want nothing more than for them to be blessed and protected by God. I want them to know their heavenly Father's presence and experience His grace, which I know will ultimately lead them to receive His peace.

But if I'm honest, it's harder for me to believe it for myself. Does God really turn His face toward me like a Father who is over-the-top in love with His daughter? Does He look at me like I look at my kids, knowing I would do anything to help them thrive, grow, flourish, and mature?

Yes. Yes, He does. And He looks at you that way too.

"See what great love the Father has given us that we should be called God's children—and we are!" (1 John 3:1).

Understanding our identity as God's children is critical to our experience of His peace. In Matthew 18, Jesus's disciples ask Him, "So who is the greatest in the kingdom of heaven?" Jesus answers by calling over a small child and then calling His followers to adopt childlike faith and humility. Jesus then goes on to say this:

> See to it that you don't despise one of these little ones, because I tell you that in heaven their angels continually view the face of my Father in heaven. What do you think? If someone has a hundred sheep, and one of them goes astray, won't he leave the ninety-nine on the hillside and go and search for the stray? And if he finds it, truly I tell you, he rejoices over that sheep more than over the ninety-nine that did not go astray. In the same way, it is not the will of your Father in heaven that one of these little ones perish. (vv. 10–14)

This is how God feels about His children. His love pursues them. His love protects them. His love goes after each child, each lamb, until it is safe in His arms.

How does Jesus's description of the Father's love in Matthew 18:10–14 mirror the prophecy about Jesus we read yesterday from Isaiah 40:11? What does this tell you about the reliability of God's Word and His character?

_____

_____

_____

_____

Read Matthew 7:9–11. How does Jesus use the analogy of a father and his children in this passage? What comes to mind when you consider "how much more" God will give you?

_____

_____

_____

_____

Reading about being a child of God can stir different reactions based on our personal upbringing. If you had a loving, protective, and supportive father, then it's likely that you relate strongly to the image of God as a good Father. But if your dad was absent, abusive, critical, or dismissive, it might be hard for you to believe or identify with God as a loving Father. If you find yourself bristling with this father/daughter language or doubting that you could be loved as a child unconditionally, take a moment to pause in prayer. Pour out your heart to God. Be honest about your fears and questions and hang-ups. He already knows your story. Let Him minister to your heart with His truth.

Psalm 27:10 says, "Even if my father and mother abandon me, the LORD cares for me." No matter what our upbringing was like, if we have accepted Jesus Christ as our Lord and Savior—acknowledging our sin and accepting His gift of grace and forgiveness—then we are children of God (John 1:12). And this we can be assured of—God gives His children good gifts!

Look up James 1:17–18. What does God give us? What does it say God does *not* do?

_____

_____

_____

_____

Let's unpack a few of God's good gifts together by reading Romans 8:14–17:

> For all who are led by the Spirit of God are children of God. So you have not received a spirit that makes you fearful slaves. Instead, you received God's Spirit when he adopted you as his own children. Now we call him, "Abba, Father." For his Spirit joins with our spirit to affirm that we are God's children. And since we are his children, we are his heirs. In fact, together with Christ we are heirs of God's glory. But if we are to share his glory, we must also share his suffering. (NLT)

First, God gives us the gift of His Spirit. The Spirit who leads us, who makes us God's adopted children. Next, He gives us the gift of calling Him "Abba, Father." This shows intimacy and endearment. God is inviting us into a close relationship with Him. He is a compassionate and comforting Father, not a distant and stoic ruler. And finally, God gives us the gift of being heirs with Christ. We inherit God's glory! Our eternal salvation is secure in Him.

Like we talked about yesterday, our suffering has purpose and can bring us closer to Jesus, who also suffered in this world. But while our pain is ultimately temporary, our position in God's family as beloved daughters will last forever.

His peace will last forever.

> What assurance does Jesus give His disciples in John 14:1–4? How does thinking about what God is preparing for you in the future help you to experience greater peace today?

_____

_____

_____

_____

SCRIPTURE MEMORY MOMENT

Write out 2 Corinthians 1:3 and think about what it means for God to be your merciful Father. Write down any additional adjectives or descriptions of Him that you want to hold close to your heart this week.

A PRAYER FOR TODAY

ABBA, FATHER, *thank You for loving me and choosing to adopt me into Your family. Thank You for pursuing me with the tenacity of a shepherd who goes after a lost sheep. I know I am safe in Your arms. I know my future is secure in You. When I'm tempted to worry about today or fear tomorrow, remind me that Your Spirit is within me and Your face is shining upon me. May Your peace and presence in my life keep growing! Amen.*

All praise to God, the Father of our Lord Jesus Christ. God is our merciful Father and the source of all comfort. He comforts us in all our troubles so that we can comfort others. When they are troubled, we will be able to give them the same comfort God has given us.

2 Corinthians 1:3–4 NLT

Have you ever been able to come alongside someone in a pain or trial that you previously experienced? How did receiving God's comfort enable you to comfort another?

We understand that we are children of God—wholly loved and adopted into His family. We get that the troubles we face in this world are temporary compared to God's eternal plan, which includes the joy of a fully restored relationship with Him and accepting our inheritance as His daughters. We know that the peace of God surpasses all understanding and that it's available to us today, in every circumstance, because the Holy Spirit is our constant guide, counselor, and advocate.

So now what? What does God desire for us to do with the peace He pours out in our lives? Simply put, share it with others.

Like so many of his letters, Paul begins 2 Corinthians with a prayer of peace: "May God our Father and the Lord Jesus Christ give you grace and peace" (1:2 NLT). Right out of the gate, Paul is pointing people to the source of true peace.

He then makes an observation that our hearts are well acquainted with by now: "All praise to God, the Father of our Lord Jesus Christ. God is our merciful Father and *the source of all comfort*" (1:3 NLT). Not praise to Netflix bingeing or Amazon Prime free shipping. Not praise to climbing the corporate ladder or paying off debt. Not even praise to Sunday afternoon naps, snuggles from a child, or a beautiful sunset. The only one worthy of our praise is God! The only one who can provide the peace and comfort our souls were created to receive is God.

Where have you looked for comfort and peace? Did those sources deliver what you were hoping for?

_____

_____

_____

_____

The only one worthy of our praise is God! The only one who can provide the peace and comfort our souls were created to receive is God.

Continue reading 2 Corinthians 1:4–7. What does Paul say is a purpose of our troubles? What does God promise to do through our suffering?

_____

_____

_____

_____

One way to confirm the meaning of Scripture is to see how one passage interrelates with and is reflected in other passages. If you're still wondering whether your current suffering has meaning or God could use you for His purpose, look at Romans 8:28: "And we know that God causes everything to work together for the good of those who love God and are called according to his purpose for them" (NLT). Notice that it doesn't say God works in all things just for our individual good. It doesn't say that God uses the seemingly shiny or proper or spiritual things in our lives. No, this passage shows a bigger story at work! God is moving and uses _everything_ for our collective good.

God does not work in isolation. Our stories are intertwined. What He's doing in my life has ripple effects in the lives of my friends and children and coworkers. That pain God is redeeming in your life, that door He is closing, that crisis He is rescuing you from has a direct impact on your life—but by His grace, it is also part of His plans for someone else's good too.

In our opening story this week, Bonnie shared about her battle with anxiety and how she has experienced God's peace and comfort through it. And guess what? As a personal friend, Bonnie has been uniquely equipped to comfort me in my own struggle with anxiety. Because she understands the struggle _and_ she has seen God meet her there, Bonnie has been able to point me to the truth and peace of Christ time and time again. I do not wish this trial for my friend, but I am thankful for how God has powerfully used Bonnie's suffering to make her a messenger of His peace, hope, and comfort.

Who has comforted you in a hard circumstance or season? Who in your life is struggling today and needs the kind of comfort from God that you understand?

_____

_____

_____

_____

_____

Paul concludes 2 Corinthians with words that are as timely for us today as they were for the original readers: "Dear brothers and sisters, I close my letter with these last words: Be joyful. Grow to maturity. Encourage each other. Live in harmony and peace. Then the God of love and peace will be with you" (13:11 NLT).

God pours out His peace to us and asks us to steward the gift well. Let's close today by meditating on God's Word and asking Him to lead us in applying what we've learned.

Be joyful. What will you choose joy in today?

_____

_____

_____

Grow to maturity. How is God asking you to keep growing? (Doing this Bible study is a fantastic way to invest in your spiritual growth and maturity. So be encouraged!)

_____

_____

_____

_____

Encourage each other. Who can you encourage today? Who can you point to God's peace?

_____

_____

_____

_____

Live in harmony and peace. What does this look like in your life right now?

_____

_____

_____

_____

Then the God of love and peace will be with you. Where do you see God's love and peace in your life? Look for Him. He is with you.

_____

_____

_____

_____

SCRIPTURE MEMORY MOMENT

Write out 2 Corinthians 1:3 and praise God for the comfort you have received from Him. If you have time, write the verse three more times in your journal.

A PRAYER FOR TODAY

GOD, *thank You for working through all things for the good of those who love You. Thank You for loving me through Your Word, through Your Spirit, through Your presence, and through the comfort of others. Help me to see opportunities to care for someone else this week. Help me to share the peace and comfort You have given me. May I continually turn back to You—the true source of everything I need. Amen.*

But I trust in your unfailing love.
    I will rejoice because you have rescued me.
I will sing to the LORD
    because he is good to me.

                          Psalm 13:5-6 NLT

What stands in the way of your joy and peace today? How has God rescued you? Does thinking about His goodness in your life (past or present) affect your current perspective?

_____

_____

_____

_____

At this point in our study, I think it's good to circle back to the truth that growing in peace doesn't equate to an absence of troubles. We know this. But sometimes it's easy to let that slippery religious lie sneak into our minds that says, "If you really trusted God, you wouldn't struggle."

Our goal through this study is right there in the title—to position ourselves as students of God's Word, surrendered to the Spirit's guidance and transforming power, so that God can *create in me* (and you!) *a heart of peace.* But it's a process, right? Peace is a day-by-day, moment-by-moment outpouring of God's goodness.

There's no doubt God has moved in your life and worked in your heart through these past five weeks. You're not the same woman you were when you began this journey. But if you're tempted to believe that you "should" be over your doubts or fears or insecurities by now, that you "should *not*" be bothered by life's hardships and troubles, then I want to tell you to take a deep breath and reexamine God's Word.

We've talked before about how the Psalms demonstrate that a relationship with God can be full of both joy and lament, sorrow and hope. Psalm 13, a psalm of David, is that kind of model.

> O LORD, how long will you forget me? Forever?
>   How long will you look the other way?
> How long must I struggle with anguish in my soul,
>   with sorrow in my heart every day?
>   How long will my enemy have the upper hand?
> Turn and answer me, O LORD my God!
>   Restore the sparkle to my eyes, or I will die.
> Don't let my enemies gloat, saying, "We have defeated him!"
>   Don't let them rejoice at my downfall.
> But I trust in your unfailing love.
>   I will rejoice because you have rescued me.
> I will sing to the LORD
>   because he is good to me. (NLT)

Verses 1–4 show David's honest distress. He openly wonders if God has forgotten about him. He admits that his soul is in anguish. These verses have no fake smiles or shiny filters. David is raw and real before God.

Then verses 5–6 show a progression toward hope. Despite how bleak his circumstances look, in the middle of feeling fragile and fearful, David resolves to trust God. Trusting leads to joy. Joy leads to calling out God's goodness.

Though the word *peace* isn't used in Psalm 13, what evidence do you find that David's heart was at peace?

Use Psalm 13 as a model for writing your own psalm. Don't worry about sounding poetic. Just begin by telling God your honest questions and what you're struggling with, and conclude with your own declaration of trust.

The impact of God's peace in our lives is not that we cease to be affected by trials but that we keep turning to God and choosing to receive His peace in our trials. Again, this is why it is so crucial for us to spend time in Scripture. We must rehearse the truth.

Jesus understands how people need to be taught the same lesson again and again, using different words and examples, so that the truth can actually sink into their hearts and reframe their worldly perspective with His peace. Listen to Jesus's teaching about trusting God's care:

> That is why I tell you not to worry about everyday life—whether you have enough food and drink, or enough clothes to wear. Isn't life more than food, and your body more than clothing? Look at the birds. They don't plant or harvest or store food in

> barns, for your heavenly Father feeds them. And aren't you far more valuable to him than they are? Can all your worries add a single moment to your life?
>
> And why worry about your clothing? Look at the lilies of the field and how they grow. They don't work or make their clothing, yet Solomon in all his glory was not dressed as beautifully as they are. And if God cares so wonderfully for wildflowers that are here today and thrown into the fire tomorrow, he will certainly care for you. Why do you have so little faith? (Matt. 6:25–30 NLT)

Look at the birds. Look at the lilies. Jesus knows how the things in front of us can seem most real. The flooded basement. The broken ankle. The demeaning boss. The unresolved conflict. He knows that what we can see often has the biggest impact on the peace (or lack thereof) we feel. We can believe God is loving and trustworthy, but when the credit card bill or angry text message is staring us in the face, our humanity causes us to zero in on that thing.

It's for this reason that Jesus says to look at what we can see. *You can see the sparrows. You can see the wildflowers. Observe how the Father cares for them. Let their presence be a continual reminder of how much more God cares for you.*

Read Matthew 10:29–31. How do these examples show that God values and cares for you?

_____

_____

_____

_____

Jesus concludes His lesson in Matthew 6 with this poignant encouragement:

> So don't worry about these things, saying, "What will we eat? What will we drink? What will we wear?" These things dominate the thoughts of unbelievers, but your heavenly Father already knows all your needs. Seek the Kingdom of God above all else, and live righteously, and he will give you everything you need.
> So don't worry about tomorrow, for tomorrow will bring its own worries. Today's trouble is enough for today. (vv. 31–34 NLT)

Your heavenly Father already knows all your needs. Full stop.

This is a picture of a God who knows you. He knit you together in your mother's womb and knows every hair on your head. He is mindful of what you went through last year and He's aware of what tomorrow holds. His intimate knowledge of you is a direct reflection of His love, care, and compassion.

Do you need a fresh outpouring of God's peace today? Go outside and look up at the birds. Take a walk and find a flower to gaze at. Open God's Word and ask Him to remind you again that He is near. The evidence of His care is all around. Keep looking.

Read Psalm 4. How does it show a similar pattern to what we saw earlier in Psalm 13? How do you feel reading the resolution in verse 8?

_____

_____

_____

_____

SCRIPTURE MEMORY MOMENT

Test yourself on 2 Corinthians 1:3. Try to say it out loud and write it from memory. As we move into the final week of our study, hide these words in your heart and reflect on them often. Perhaps write 2 Corinthians 1:3 on a sticky note and put it somewhere you'll see it every day.

A PRAYER FOR TODAY

GOD, *I'm so grateful I can be honest with You. Thank You for loving me in the middle of my doubts and questions and fears. And thank You for giving me reminders through Your Word and through creation of how much You care for me. Help me to receive Your peace today. Pour it out, Jesus. Let it wash over every crevice of my heart. I love You. Amen.*

PEACE IS OUR PURPOSE

The peace of God is not only an internal experience, a gift and by-product of submitting ourselves to the Holy Spirit's guidance and work in our lives; peace is also a challenge and an invitation. Peace is the path of Jesus, and we're called to follow Him in it so that others may come to know Him too.

Peace is a mark of the mature believer. Living at peace with others is not something we can do by our own strength—because let's face it, we're all sinners with enough baggage to overload any luggage cart. But living with the peace of God and extending that peace to others will set us apart—and will set our hearts free to live out our calling as God's daughters.

Today's story by (in)courage writer Lucretia Berry gives us a glimpse into how crucial peace is when we're fulfilling our purpose for Jesus. Lucretia is an anti-racism educator who creates safe learning spaces for individuals, churches, and schools to understand and move toward racial healing. But as we'll see, walking in step with God's calling isn't without resistance. As you read Lucretia's story, consider how you need to be immersed in God's vision for your life.

A Story of Peace

The lies land like punches to the stomach. Accusers frantically flail word bombs like Molotov cocktails. People who've never met me weaponize words, forging them into arrows to pierce me. Writhing in pain, tending to my wounds, I ponder how they can boldly attack me in the name of Jesus and for the sake of Christianity. I've been called a false prophet, and my ministry and mission have been judged as "not Christian," "liberal," "progressive," "Marxist," and whatever other shame-inducing, reductive jargon du jour is curated from a place of fear. Even a fellow parishioner invited me to coffee with a prerequisite: "I want to get to know you better, BUT I don't want to talk about your ministry!" I thought, *How is she going to get to know me, hear me, or truly see me without understanding the invitation I received from the Holy Spirit—the very essence of God—to co-labor in racial healing?*

Sadly, I have grown accustomed to such resistance to the holy, deep trust walk required to heal our collective wounds of racism. Nevertheless, it still stings each time people hurl stones—especially because they attempt to validate their stone-throwing with the gospel. The pain lingers like an echo within. The ache bounces from my heart to my psyche and back again, as I attempt to comprehend their hostility, their audacity, their source. I wish I had authority over the wave of pain—to command it to cease as fiercely as it consumes me. I wish I had a heart of hardened steel so I wouldn't feel the hurt so deeply. I wish I didn't care what people thought about me. But I do care. And I have learned that each wave of pain takes me to a place where the softness of my heart is essential.

A couple years ago, I was pummeled by Audrey's (a pseudonym) accusatory reply to one of my social media shares. Not only was I offended by what Audrey said to me and about me to anyone who read her comments, but I was also angry that her verbal violence is normal. A quick glance through our historical attempts to overcome racial injustice reveals a disheartening pattern. Abolitionists were labeled "agitators." Reverend Dr. Martin Luther King Jr. and other civil rights advocates were vilified as "communists." And Audrey condemned my educational initiatives for racial healing as "anti-White" and "not Christian." I wondered if Audrey realized that she was inciting shame and blame to wrongly accuse me of shaming and blaming.

I peered through Audrey's words and saw her defensive posturing. I saw her outrage. I discerned her fear. I could have escaped my pain by ignoring Audrey's insults. After all, others left many encouraging comments that could have eclipsed her condemning accusations. But the pain clung to my ribs and would not let me go. I began to pray for Audrey—for her eyes and heart to be opened to see and know God's heart for repair. As I prayed for Audrey to gain a heart for healing, I discerned an absence of peace. Audrey's offensive maneuvers were motivated by fear, not peace. And I was praying for her from a reservoir of trauma, not a wellspring of peace. Void of peace, vision is cloudy.

I sat in pain, in limbo, with no peace. Without peace, hopelessness is inevitable. Healing does not happen in hostility. I was stalled.

When Hannah, the mother of the Old Testament prophet Samuel, believed she was barren, she traveled to Shiloh to pray for God to bless her with a child (1 Sam. 1:1–18). Shiloh was the most important Israelite shrine at that time, a sanctuary known as a place of peace. When Hannah poured out her heart in prayer, Eli the priest answered, "Go in peace, and may the God of Israel grant you what you have asked of him." Soon after that, Hannah became pregnant with Samuel.

I imagine that Hannah walked home from Shiloh in peace, not yet pregnant but actively shopping for maternity clothes. Peace is not simply a feeling of calm or the absence of chaos. Peace is fully immersing ourselves in God's vision. Peace exists when the seed rests in intelligent soil, knowing that the soil is cultivating it. Peace is the garden where hope takes root. I have learned that to be an extension of God's vision, peace and I must be each other's dwelling places.

I paused my requests for God to take away my pain from Audrey's accusations. In the quiet of my soul, I clearly heard God's vision for my next steps for serving the divine invitation to foster racial healing. Like Hannah, who was told "Go in peace," I was no longer stifled by pain and frustration. In peace, I was able to move forward. In peace, God led me specifically to create a peace-informed learning space that serves thousands of students who need a garden in which to grow.

People often ask me, "How do you do this difficult work?" After a few times, I realized their question was rooted in frustration and hopelessness. When people ask me that question, they are actually looking for a life-giving, hope-filled vision to hold. They are looking for peace.

Perhaps your "Audrey" looks different from mine. Perhaps weapons are formed against you for other reasons. Let's remember that when we walk in purpose, not everyone will like us, and many times we'll get hurt. But even when we experience pain, if we fully immerse ourselves in God's vision with peace as our purpose, we can move forward in clarity and with confidence.

—LUCRETIA BERRY

When has a critical voice become louder than God's voice in your life? How did focusing on defending your personhood or position affect your peace?

_____

_____

_____

_____

Lucretia wrote, "Void of peace, vision is cloudy." When has this been true for you?

_____

_____

_____

_____

Read Mark 8:22–25. Did Jesus bring healing all at once? What does this example of regaining vision in stages tell you about how God cares for people? Consider how your spiritual vision is more or less clear today than in the past. Write out a prayer for the area of your life you need Jesus to touch and bring greater clarity and peace.

SCRIPTURE MEMORY MOMENT

This week's memory verses are Ephesians 4:2–3. Write out the verses in your journal (as printed here from the NIV or from your favorite translation). Throughout the week, commit these words to memory as you ask God to create in you a heart of peace.

Be completely humble and gentle; be patient, bearing with one another in love. Make every effort to keep the unity of the Spirit through the bond of peace.

A PRAYER FOR TODAY

FATHER, SON, HOLY SPIRIT, *thank You for being with me and in me today. I want to be a woman who walks in step with You. Not out of fear or pride or defensiveness but with humility, gentleness, and confidence that I am doing the work You've given me to do. Spirit, You are peace! May You continue to help me see what You see and bond my heart to You. Amen.*

Do not repay anyone evil for evil. Give careful thought to do what is honorable in everyone's eyes. If possible, as far as it depends on you, live at peace with everyone.

Romans 12:17–18

When have you had the opportunity to repay evil for evil? Did you choose the path of payback or peace? How did that turn out?

Let's just get the obvious out in the open: living at peace with others isn't easy—especially when we've been hurt. Yet Scripture is abundantly clear that we are called to forgive others as Christ forgave us and to live at peace with others (Col. 3:12–15). To this end, Paul urged believers in Rome, "If possible, as far as it depends on you, live at peace with everyone" (Rom. 12:18). Let's break this down:

- *If possible*—an acknowledgment that *sometimes* peace between people may not be possible.

- *As far as it depends on you*—when it comes to peace-living, we have personal responsibility.
- *Live at peace with everyone*—not with those who are kind and loving, not with those you agree with on every issue, but with *everyone*.

It's tempting to believe that following these instructions is too tall an order—especially in today's culture. When vicious social media comments are as common as likes and shares, when political divisions run deep and racial violence is on the upswing, it's tempting to put all of life's hard relationships in the "peace is impossible" column.

But there's a reason the Bible is full of commands to be peacemakers. First, it's important to God's heart. Second, it's crucial to living out our call as God's beloved children. As a fruit of the Spirit, peace marks us. It makes us stand out so that the spotlight can rightly shine on God. Because as we learned last week, peace is an outpouring, and it's only by His strength and grace that we can be equipped to fulfill our purpose.

> Read Romans 12:9–13. The Christian Standard Bible says, "Let love be without hypocrisy" and "Take the lead in honoring one another." The New International Version translates it as "Love must be sincere" and "Honor one another above yourselves." How do you think these ideas of love and honor relate to living at peace with one another?

Continue reading Romans 12:14–16. What example from Scripture and/ or your own life demonstrates what it looks like to bless those who persecute you? (Look up Luke 6:35–36 for one example.)

_____

_____

_____

In thinking about what it looks like to live at peace and bless those who persecute you, we ought to consider the story of Joseph and his brothers. The whole heartrending, dramatic, relationally complex, and God-filled account can be found in Genesis 37–45. It's definitely worth finding the time to read the entire story.

Here's a very brief overview: Joseph was one of the twelve sons of Jacob (aka Israel). His brothers were jealous of him because he was their father's favorite. Joseph also told his family about two dreams he had in which everyone was bowing down to him, which only exacerbated their envy and anger. One day Joseph's brothers plotted to kill him, but eventually they decided to sell him to slave traders instead.

Young Joseph was taken to Egypt and became a servant for a man named Potiphar, one of Pharaoh's officers. There God blessed Joseph. He was found trustworthy and was put in charge of Potiphar's household and everything he owned. But this great favor ran dry when Potiphar's wife falsely accused Joseph of attempting to seduce her—an accusation that resulted in his imprisonment.

Fast-forward with me through more God-ordained blessings in the face of severe trials. After spending at least two years in prison, Joseph was called on to interpret a confusing dream Pharaoh had. Pharaoh then released Joseph and appointed him as second in command over all of Egypt. Through Pharaoh's dream, God had revealed to Joseph that seven years of plenty would be followed by seven years of famine. So he instituted a system for storing grain during the years of plenty to prepare for the impending scarcity.

When the famine spread across the land, people from all over the surrounding areas came to Egypt to buy grain. The lines of people waiting for a portion of grain stretched on and on. Can you guess who was in one of those lines? Joseph's brothers.

> **Put yourself in Joseph's shoes. Imagine the emotional trauma of seeing the people who intended to kill you but settled for selling you as a slave. The people responsible for years of hunger, imprisonment, and mistreatment. What would you say to them? What would you do?**

If it were me, after all those years I'd have some well-rehearsed choice words for the brothers who abandoned me. It would be only natural for Joseph to want to refuse giving even a single grain of wheat to the family who betrayed him. After all, why should he help those who caused so much suffering and hurt?

In the events that unfold after Joseph recognizes his brothers, we don't see a picture of immediate grace and forgiveness. We see a person deeply wounded by his past. We see a man trying to judge for himself whether his brothers are worthy of compassion and mercy. Joseph is not forthcoming about his identity—his brothers see him only as a high-ranking Egyptian leader, not the young man they once sold into slavery.

But as the story progresses, we see evidence of God working in Joseph's heart—reminding him of the endless mercy and favor poured out to him. Eventually, Joseph reveals who he is, and instead of scorn and judgment, Joseph extends peace to those who once counted him disposable.

> Then Joseph said to his brothers, "Please, come near me," and they came near. "I am Joseph, your brother," he said, "the one you sold into Egypt. And now don't be grieved or angry with yourselves for selling me here, because God sent me ahead of you to preserve life. For the famine has been in the land these two years, and there will be five more years without plowing or harvesting. God sent me ahead of you to establish you as a remnant within the land and to keep you alive by a great deliverance." (Gen. 45:4–7)

Joseph then invites his brothers and all their families to relocate to Egypt—not just to survive the famine but to thrive together.

Living at peace with one another requires us to remember the peace we've received from God—the forgiveness He has given and the unearned favor He has shown each one of us. For God did not treat us as our sins deserve. Instead, He calls us family—beloved children.

When peace feels too hard and personal retribution seems right, may we let God's forgiveness lead us forward.

Read Psalm 103:1–14 and write down every description of God. What does He do with our sins? How can God's compassion in your life move you to build a bridge toward peace with someone?

SCRIPTURE MEMORY MOMENT

Write out Ephesians 4:2–3. How might God be asking you to humble yourself and seek peace? Now text this passage to a friend who might be encouraged by it. Invite her to memorize it with you!

A PRAYER FOR TODAY

JESUS, *I'll be honest: sometimes the path of peace feels impossible. I know not every relationship can be restored—You don't ever desire to put me in harm's way. But Your Word also reminds me that what is impossible with people is possible with You. Thank You for not treating me as I deserve. Thank You for covering every mistake I've made with Your love and grace. Empower me to do the same for others today. Create in me a heart of peace. Amen.*

Above all, clothe yourselves with love, which binds us all together in perfect harmony. And let the peace that comes from Christ rule in your hearts. For as members of one body you are called to live in peace. And always be thankful.

Colossians 3:14–15 NLT

What do you think it means to let the peace of Christ rule in your heart?

_____

_____

_____

_____

"Live at peace with everyone." Paul's words from Romans 12, which we looked at yesterday, reverberate in Colossians 3: *"You are called to live in peace."* Does this mean we already know what to do so we can skim past this teaching? Not so much. When themes and specific instructions appear multiple times in Scripture, they should make our eyes focus in, our ears perk up, and our hearts open in curiosity and surrender. Repetition is a signal to pay attention, to lean in.

In the same way young children need to learn the same lesson again and again, so do we. Growth and maturity, understanding and application happen gradually. (If my kids could learn overnight to be perfectly kind, loving, and unselfish and to never argue with one another, that would be amazing! But after thirteen years of motherhood, I'm still having to repeat, model, and explain these lessons over and over.) So God, our loving Father who desires to see us grow in maturity, *continually* reminds us of the truth and gives us directions for right living.

With this in mind, let's lean in to today's teaching with expectancy that God will continue to reveal new layers of meaning and usher in fresh growth as we learn what it means to pursue peace.

Read Colossians 3:12–15. How does putting on ("clothing ourselves") with the qualities listed prepare us to live at peace with others? Is peace possible without mercy, kindness, humility, gentleness, and patience?

_____

_____

_____

_____

Whose faults do you need to make allowances for today? Do you have any unforgiveness in your heart? Read verse 13 again and remember how much God has forgiven you.

_____

_____

_____

_____

Is it a coincidence that Paul writes about forgiveness just before reminding us that we are called to live in peace? Definitely not. Like other forms of literature, Paul's letters (also called epistles) are written in an intentional progression so that ideas and instructions build upon each other.

Let's look again at Colossians 3:12–15 (NLT) and break it down this way:

> "God chose you to be the holy people he loves."

Because that is true, do this:

> "Clothe yourselves with tenderhearted mercy, kindness, humility, gentleness, and patience."

Doing that will prepare you for this:

> "Make allowance for each other's faults, and forgive anyone who offends you."

If you're having trouble doing that, do this:

> "Remember, the Lord forgave you, so you must forgive others."

Here's what all that leads to:

> "Above all, clothe yourselves with love, which binds us all together in perfect harmony."

When all of this is in place, you'll be able to:

> "Let the peace that comes from Christ rule in your hearts."

Why do you need to do this?

> "For as members of one body you are called to live in peace."

And don't forget:

> "Always be thankful."

Every part of God's Word is intentional and helps us live out our purpose. Individual words or sentences are not meant to be cherry-picked according to how palatable we deem them. Certainly Paul would have intended his letter to be read from start to finish—not cut up and passed around so that each person got just a snippet. We need the whole context.

That said, living out the whole context isn't easy. It isn't easy to put on gentleness with a brash coworker who makes demeaning comments. It isn't easy to put on patience with a child who has deliberately pressed every one of your buttons and is wearing you down just to get their way. It's not easy to make allowances for a friend's faults when you think she should know better, or to forgive an offense that cuts deep to your heart.

But, friend, easy isn't the point. Nor are we asked to live these instructions by our own strength.

> **True peace isn't something we have to manufacture or strive after. Jesus is the source, and we have full access.**

Read Psalm 29:11 and Hebrews 12:11. What does God give His people? What happens when we allow ourselves to be disciplined and trained by God's Word?

_____

_____

_____

_____

Colossians 3:15 reveals the source of our peace—of our everything, really: Christ! "Let the peace *that comes from Christ* rule in your hearts." Not peace from being a pushover or avoiding conflict. Not peace from being a good person or getting everyone to like you. Peace that comes from Christ! Isn't this good news? True peace isn't something we have to manufacture or strive after. Jesus is the source, and we have full access.

The growth progression we looked at above is reciprocal too. When we let Christ's peace have full authority in our hearts—that is, Christ's peace gets to dictate what takes root and what gets rooted out—*then* we will also be better able to clothe ourselves like Christ and forgive others.

If that still sounds too vague, think of it like this: Imagine Jesus is the gatekeeper of your heart. When worry and fear and bitterness come knocking, Jesus kindly denies them access. But He swings the gate wide open for love and forgiveness. Do you get the picture?

Jesus doesn't force His peace on us. We have to let it in and let it rule.

Remember this week's opening story? Lucretia shared about being cut down by a racially charged social media comment. She wrote, "I sat in pain, in limbo, with no peace. Without peace, hopelessness is inevitable. Healing does not happen in hostility. I was stalled." Remember Joseph's story? He ultimately forgave his brothers, but the path forward was not without pain and hostility. Joseph tested his brothers to see if they had changed. He wept as he remembered what they had done to him.

Indeed, healing does not happen in hostility. Healing happens when we let the peace that comes from Jesus rule our hearts and lead us to respond to others with mercy, gentleness, and forgiveness.

There's no doubt that Joseph gave thanks for the way God brought restoration to his family and for the gift of seeing his earthly father again. For Lucretia, experiencing God's peace didn't mean restoring her relationship with Audrey, but it did mean she was able to move forward with greater clarity and freedom in pursuing her purpose as a peacemaker.

When we let the peace of Christ rule in our hearts, we can live at peace with others, with ourselves, and with our God. Indeed, that is a reason to always be thankful.

Read Psalm 85, paying special attention to verse 8. What does God do for His people, and what does He ask us to do? How can you listen carefully to the Lord this week?

SCRIPTURE MEMORY MOMENT

Write out Ephesians 4:2–3 and think about how you can bear with someone in love today.

A PRAYER FOR TODAY

JESUS, *what would I do without You? Without You, I would be trapped in my sin. Without You, I would be stuck in unforgiveness toward others. Without You, I would be hopeless, chasing after peace that I could never secure by my own strength. But in You, my Lord, I have peace. Help me this week to cover myself with Your character. Keep growing me in gentleness and humility. Keep rooting out bitterness and hopelessness in my heart. I give You authority over my life. I am Yours. Make me Your peacemaker. Amen.*

DAY 4

Keep your tongue from evil
and your lips from deceitful speech.
Turn away from evil and do what is good;
seek peace and pursue it.

Psalm 34:13–14

What comes to mind when you think about keeping your tongue from evil?

_____

_____

_____

_____

In our day-to-day lives, most of us aren't thinking about being evil. We are women who love the Lord. We're busy scrubbing toilets and making breakfast. We're volunteering in our community, going to Bible study, calling our friends, rocking babies, rocking singleness, loving our neighbors, encouraging a coworker. Are we really so turned toward evil that we would need to consider turning away from it?

We _know_ there is no such thing as big or little sins. In God's eyes, sin is sin. Anyone who stumbles on one point of God's law is guilty of breaking all of it (see James 2:10). Yet from our human perspective, it's still easy to categorize sin and evil on a sliding scale of what's most socially palatable. We may not outright spew lies or blatantly deceive someone, but do we embellish the truth to make ourselves look good? We may not outright slander another, but are we critical when someone rubs us the wrong way or makes a choice we don't agree with and we're not shy about saying so?

For nearly six weeks, we have sought God through His Word and asked Him to create in us a heart of peace. Why? So that we can go about our days feeling calm, centered, and less anxious? Sure, that's a great by-product. But the point of God's peace isn't so we can hoard it for our own comfort and assurance. No, His peace is for a purpose—an invitation to partner with Him as peacemakers. Peace bringers. Peace ambassadors and advocates. Adopted daughters and coheirs with the Prince of Peace. Our purpose is to seek peace and pursue it so others will know God's love, join His family, and flourish.

But there can be barriers to our purpose. Things we may not even be aware of. David prayed, "Search me, God, and know my heart; test me and know my concerns. See if there is any offensive way in me; lead me in the everlasting way" (Ps. 139:23–24).

Pause and make this your prayer as you begin today's study.

God's peace is for a purpose—an invitation to partner with Him as peacemakers. Peace bringers. Peace ambassadors and advocates. Adopted daughters and coheirs with the Prince of Peace. Our purpose is to seek peace and pursue it so others will know God's love, join His family, and flourish.

Look up the following verses and jot down a note about each passage. How does what we say affect others?

Proverbs 12:18 _____

_____

Proverbs 15:1 _____

_____

Ephesians 4:29 _____

_____

James 1:26 _____

_____

Read Psalm 34:11–14 and think about the progression of the psalmist's instructions: listen to the Lord's teaching, enjoy a good life, keep your tongue from evil, do good, and pursue peace. How does each idea relate to the next? How is pursuing peace dependent on the preceding instructions?

_____

_____

_____

_____

If the Bible were being written today, I imagine it might also include commands to keep your fingers from typing unkind and careless words and to guard your time on social media because harsh accusations make tempers flare. These are some of the ways we face the temptation of evil every day. It's no secret that we live in a culture where people spew unkind words online to friends and strangers alike that they would probably never say face-to-face.

Even among Christians, our words have become like divisive swords poised to tear into those who don't act, think, believe, or respond to current events in the manner we deem appropriate or right. Over and over on Facebook, Twitter, Instagram, and online articles, Christ-followers skewer one another and seemingly rejoice when the so-called offender bleeds.

The only blood that brings peace is the blood of Jesus.

Hold up what you see in today's culture against what you read in Scripture:

> Therefore I, a prisoner for serving the Lord, beg you to lead a life worthy of your calling, for you have been called by God. Always be humble and gentle. Be patient with each other, making allowance for each other's faults because of your love. Make every effort to keep yourselves united in the Spirit, binding yourselves together with peace. (Eph. 4:1–3 NLT)

Paul penned this call to peace not as someone for whom conflict and hardship were hypothetical. This call to humility and gentleness came from a man who had been imprisoned, spat upon, and torn apart with whips and with words. Paul knew that the only solution for humans who tear each other apart is to bind ourselves together again with the peace of God.

Looking at Ephesians 4:1–3 again, what do you think it means to "lead a life worthy of your calling"? What does Colossians 3:15 say we're called to?

A big part of Paul's ministry was spent helping believers to stop fighting with one another and to stop making minor issues—like what to eat and drink—into major issues that caused disunity. The interesting thing is that Paul never preached an "everyone should agree with everyone on everything" message. For example, he knew that Christians from a Jewish background would still feel the need to uphold the practice of circumcision, whereas gentile converts to Christianity would not. Debating which perspective was right or wrong was insignificant compared to focusing on what was truly important. Paul writes, "Circumcision does not matter and uncircumcision does not matter. Keeping God's commands is what matters" (1 Cor. 7:19).

Sometimes I wonder what God thinks as He watches His children quarrel. Does He feel the same way I do when I hear my kids bickering about inconsequential things? My sons are pros at making mountains out of molehills, and sometimes I just want to yell, "It doesn't matter whose turn it is to empty the dishwasher or whether those actually were your socks! Can't you just love one another and be kind because you are brothers?"

Indeed, I want my children to climb down off their pedestals of pride and stubbornness. I want them to care less about being right and more about caring for others. I want them to be humble and gentle and, yes, peaceful. I can understand why God desires the same from us.

Hebrews 12:14–15 says, "Work at living in peace with everyone, and work at living a holy life, for those who are not holy will not see the Lord. Look after each other so that none of you fails to receive the grace of God. Watch out that no poisonous root of bitterness grows up to trouble you, corrupting many" (NLT).

To live a life worthy of our calling as God's daughters means pursuing peace and looking after one another. By God's grace, we can do it.

Read Hebrews 12:14–15 again. How are living at peace and living a holy life connected? Why do you think the writer uses the verb phrase "work at"? Who can you look after today?

SCRIPTURE MEMORY MOMENT

Write out Ephesians 4:2–3. What does the bond of peace look like in your life? If you have time, write the verses three more times in your journal.

A PRAYER FOR TODAY

GOD, *thank You for another day to cultivate a heart of peace. Living at peace with my brothers and sisters isn't easy. I confess it's more comfortable to point fingers and cast blame than to humble myself and love someone I don't agree with. But I want to be a woman of peace. I want to live worthy of the calling You've placed on my life. Show me what that looks like today, right where I am. Amen.*

DAY 5

Blessed are the peacemakers, for they will be called children of God.

Matthew 5:9 NIV

Think about all the ways you identify yourself—roles you play, relationships you hold. How much do "peacemaker" and "child of God" shape your identity?

_____

_____

_____

_____

Jesus's first recorded message is known as the Sermon on the Mount. At this point, Jesus has already called His first disciples and is traveling throughout Galilee, healing people from every sickness and disease. Seeing the large crowds following Him, Jesus retreats to a mountain and sits down to teach His disciples. He begins his famous sermon with what are called the Beatitudes, a series of eight blessings that identify what the kingdom of God looks like on earth.

The Prince of Peace—the promised Messiah who came to both rule and redeem earth—wants His followers to know what He values, what they can expect from Him. Does He praise warriors and promise to raise up a mighty army? Does He esteem religious leaders and elevate them to positions of authority? Here's what He says:

> Blessed are the poor in spirit,
>   for theirs is the kingdom of heaven.
> Blessed are those who mourn,
>   for they will be comforted.
> Blessed are the meek,
>   for they will inherit the earth.
> Blessed are those who hunger and thirst for righteousness,
>   for they will be filled.
> Blessed are the merciful,
>   for they will be shown mercy.
> Blessed are the pure in heart,
>   for they will see God.
> Blessed are the peacemakers,
>   for they will be called children of God.
> Blessed are those who are persecuted because of
>   righteousness,
>   for theirs is the kingdom of heaven. (Matt. 5:3–10 NIV)

Do you hear the echo of Jesus's words in the Scripture passages we've studied for the past six weeks? Comfort. Mercy. Peace. He offers no accolades for the strong and self-sufficient. Jesus isn't propping up the proud and powerful. Instead, He blesses those who are poor in spirit, assuring them that their heavenly inheritance is rich and secure. Jesus cares not about our might but about our hearts. Not our self-made perfection but our hunger for His righteousness.

Jesus came as the ultimate peacemaker, inviting both Jews and gentiles—that is, God's original chosen people and the rest of humanity—into His family. *Be a peacemaker like Me, sister, and you will be God's daughter.*

From all you've learned in this study, what does it mean to be a peace-maker? Write your definition as a personal purpose statement.

_____

_____

_____

_____

Read Ephesians 2:11–17, which describes the early church's ongoing conflict between Jewish and gentile believers. What did Christ do for the people? How should Jesus's example of peacemaking affect how we live and relate to others?

_____

_____

_____

_____

Jesus removed the separation between Jews and gentiles. He made two groups one. This may not seem like a big deal to us today. From our historically removed perspective, it's simple to see that God's love extends to everyone. If now we are all under grace instead of the law, what's the big deal if everyone doesn't follow the same customs?

Well . . . transfer this scenario to something that hits closer to home. Think about other Christians who are part of a different church denomination or political party than you. Now apply the words of Ephesians 2:14: "For he himself is our peace, who has made the two groups one and has destroyed the barrier, the dividing wall of hostility" (NIV). Let that sink in.

The beautiful thing about Jesus is that He doesn't ask us to do anything He hasn't first done Himself.

Who do you feel divided from by a wall of hostility? Picture that person or group of people in your mind. Then picture Jesus on the cross—dying for you *and* for them. How could this picture lead you to pursue peace?

_____

_____

_____

_____

The beautiful thing about Jesus is that He doesn't ask us to do anything He hasn't first done Himself.

Love as God has loved you. (John 13:34)

Forgive one another as Christ has forgiven you. (Eph. 4:32)

Comfort others with the comfort you've received. (2 Cor. 1:3–4)

Live at peace with everyone, for Jesus is our peace. (Rom. 12:18; Eph. 2:14)

The world tells us to make ourselves judge and jury for those who disagree with us. Keep your distance. Don't like, follow, or have dinner with those who hold different political and social justice stances. The world tells us to tear down those who believe and worship in a way unlike our own. To villainize and demonize and demoralize anyone who is not in our group. Turn on the evening news or scan Twitter, and you can see this is the way of the world. But let's be clear: this is not the way of Jesus.

> But the wisdom from above is first of all pure. It is also peace loving, gentle at all times, and willing to yield to others. It is full of mercy and the fruit of good deeds. It shows no favoritism and is always sincere. And those who are peacemakers will plant seeds of peace and reap a harvest of righteousness. (James 3:17–18 NLT)

We began this study by learning that peace is a *person*. When making peace our purpose feels too hard, too heavy, too impossible, we must return to the person of Jesus. Return to His love. Return to His forgiveness. Return to His comfort. Return to His peace. Remembering what God has already accomplished on the cross and in our lives is what will give us the wisdom and strength we need to live worthy of our calling as God's daughters. Not perfect, not struggle-free—but *worthy* because God makes us so.

Be a peacemaker. Wherever you are today, plant seeds of peace—no matter how small or inconsequential they seem. God will make the harvest grow.

Read 1 Peter 3:8–12 and notice how the writer quotes Psalm 34:12–16, which we studied earlier this week. Quiet your heart and read the passage again slowly. What part of this instruction is God emphasizing to you?

_____

_____

_____

_____

SCRIPTURE MEMORY MOMENT

Test yourself on Ephesians 4:2–3. Try to say it out loud and write it from memory. Hide these words in your heart and reflect on them often. Perhaps write Ephesians 4:2–3 on a sticky note and put it somewhere you'll see it every day. When you have time, go back through all six memory passages. Continue to meditate on these truths as you move forward as a peacemaker.

A PRAYER FOR TODAY

DEAR GOD, *thank You for calling me Your child. Jesus, thank You for coming to this world to die for my sins and break down walls. Holy Spirit, thank You for working in my heart and guiding me in the way of peace. Oh, how I need You! On my own, I can't love, forgive, or pursue peace. But I am not on my own; Your power and strength are in me. Your peace is a river that never runs dry. Remind me to drink from Your living water daily. Call me to abide in You, my Prince of Peace. And use this heart of peace You've grown in me to invite others to experience Your peace too. Amen.*

ABOUT THE AUTHORS

Becky Keife is the (in)courage community manager, a popular speaker, and the author of *The Simple Difference* and the *Courageous Kindness* Bible study. Becky loves helping others truly see the people in front of them, God's lavish love for them, and His mighty power within them. She and her husband live near Los Angeles, where they enjoy hiking sunny trails with their three spirited sons. Connect with Becky on Instagram @beckykeife or at beckykeife.com.

Lucretia Berry is the creator of Brownicity.com. She is a wife, a mom of three, and a former college professor, whose passion for racial healing led her to author *What LIES Between Us: Fostering First Steps Toward Racial Healing* and *Hues of You*. Find her at brownicity.com and on Instagram @lucretiaberry.

Robin Dance is the author of *For All Who Wander*, is married to her college sweetheart, and is as Southern as sugar-shocked tea. An empty nester with a full life, she's determined to age with grace and laugh at the days to come. Connect with her at robindance.me and on Instagram @robindance.me.

Bonnie Gray is a wife, a mom to two boys, and the author of three books, including her new release, *Sweet Like Jasmine: Finding Identity in a Culture of Loneliness*. An inspirational speaker who has been featured in *Relevant Magazine* and *Christianity Today*, she's guided thousands to detox stress and experience God's love through soul care. Find her at thebonniegray.com and on Instagram @thebonniegray.

Anna E. Rendell is the (in)courage digital content manager and lives in Minnesota with her husband and four kids. She loves a good book and a great latte. Anna is the author of *Pumpkin Spice for Your Soul* and *A Moment of Christmas*. Visit her at annarendell.com and on Instagram @annaerendell.

Jen Schmidt encourages women to embrace both the beauty and the bedlam of their everyday lives at beautyandbedlam.com and on Instagram @jenschmidt_beautyandbedlam. A speaker, worship leader, and author of *Just Open the Door: How One Invitation Can Change a Generation*, Jen lives in North Carolina with her husband and five children.

(in)courage welcomes you

to a place where authentic, brave women connect deeply with God and others. Through the power of shared stories and meaningful resources, (in)courage champions women and celebrates the strength Jesus gives to live out our calling as God's daughters. Together we build community, celebrate diversity, and **become women of courage.**

Join us at **www.incourage.me**
and connect with us on social media!

New Women's Bible Study Series from the (in)courage Community

This six-week Bible study series from (in)courage pairs Scripture with story, inviting us into a deeper experience of God's Word. Packed with solid observation, interpretation, and application of Scripture, plus daily prayers and memorization, each study strengthens the partnership between us and God.